The WONDERFUL WORLD of OPRAH

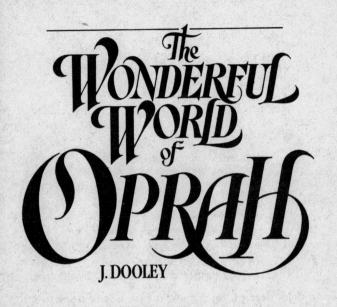

The WONDERFUL WORLD of OPRAH

J. DOOLEY

A Critic's Choice paperback
from Lorevan Publishing, Inc.
New York, New York

ISBN: 1-55547-238-9

First Critic's Choice edition: 1988

From LOREVAN PUBLISHING, INC.

Critic's Choice Paperbacks
31 E. 28th St.
New York, New York 10016

Printed in association with GAP International

Manufactured in the United States of America

Dedication:

This book is dedicated to Andee Elizabeth and Michael John.

Special thanks to Gary Brodsky, Dr. William D. Cox—
Tennessee State University, Elizabeth Dooley, Charles and
Ruth Holden, J.T. and Elsie Hunn, Michelle Gleed, Cathy
Moley, Gary Noar, and hello to Carol and Dave . . .

Contents

CHAPTER

1

part one—OW!

"I had a difficult childhood, and other people have a difficult adulthood. I think we are all victimized or feel victimized at some point in our lives, but we have to be responsible for claiming our own victories."
—OPRAH WINFREY

If you are one of the millions of viewers who watch *The Oprah Winfrey Show* regularly, then you have a good friend in show business. Oprah Winfrey is the closest thing we have to an all-around, perfect entertainer. She is stunningly beautiful, larger than life, honest, and is as warm as your grandmother's house. She is a 33 going on 34-year-old entertainment powerhouse, and she is always looking for ways to prove it. Her first introduction to the professional entertainment industry was as a live action reporter in Nashville, Tennessee; following that, she went into almost every aspect of the industry. She has proved her abilities as a broadcaster, TV journalist, talk-show host, award-winning motion picture star and, most recently, she's trying her hand at the production aspect of television film, with her upcoming ABC drama, *The Women of Brewster Place*.

Her ongoing television project, *The Oprah Winfrey Show*, is seen in more than 135 cities across the nation and it frequently leads in the all-important ratings.

Oprah Winfrey is the Queen of daytime television and rules her vast television 'queendom' with a firm, yet gentle hand. She is a big, flashy, and electrifying woman, with high ideals and highly refined talents. At the same time, she is an honest, lovable, straight-talking champion of the common folk. She is also very rich.

The story of Oprah Winfrey's incredible life is a tale of dramatic challenge and timely fortune. Once a simple farm girl, standing in the Mississippi sun, poor, except for her sincere strengths and inner drive to succeed, Oprah has managed to overcome poverty, rape, and suicidal tendencies. Grabbing the reins of her circumstances, she rode into the multi-million-dollar national treasure that she is today. She is the blur of a forward motion, honest with herself and honest with those who watch her program. People love Oprah for reasons that they never had to consider in the past when choosing a favorite talk-show host. She is very alert and coyishly cunning.

People don't just 'tune in' to *The Oprah Winfrey Show*; they think of Oprah as a friend, and they cheerfully invite her into their homes. In the imitation world of glitzy, plasticized television personalities, Oprah stands out as an example of her real-life qualities, which endears her to her viewers. She acts like a human being on her show. People aren't put off by a stiff-witted, illusory talk-show personality because she doesn't have one. She is as real as the nose on your face. Her unconventional and somewhat tragic youth has brought her a hard-earned understanding of the frequent cruelties that life sometimes offers.

Katherine Hepburn once said, "Two of an actress' greatest assets are love and pain. A great actress, even a good actress, must have plenty of both." If this is the true test of an actress' most-needed assets, then Oprah can relax; she has what it takes. Ms. Hepburn might appreciate Oprah's talents, and she would be a sensational guest on Oprah's show.

Oprah's two films, *The Color Purple* and *The Native Son*, have proven her fine-acting mettle. In her upcoming television drama, *The Women of Brewster Place*, Oprah will have the opportunity to share her talent with millions of television viewers who don't usually watch her show on TV. When the production airs on ABC, early in 1988, her fan population will grow considerably. Even though her role as Mattie Michael will be her first television starring role, Oprah's initial dramatic television debut came in the form of a short walk-on part on one of her favorite daytime soap operas, *All My Children*, in 1983.

Oprah's viewers don't always agree with the things that Oprah believes, and says on her show, but most of the time she is right on the money with them, eliciting deep-felt emotions. She and her audience often share a common-bond understanding and reasoning. One topic that Oprah and her audience seem to share in their interests is: men. With a sometimes shocking ease, Oprah surprises her audience with spontaneous questions such as, "Let me ask you women here today, 'Would you stay with a man if he could not maintain an erection, over a period of time?' " She does it with such sincere interest that she usually gets a response. Besides that, Oprah's audience isn't scared away by this type of insisive question. They are used to this kind of rope-in-teeth questioning. That's why they watch the show—they expect it. Oprah's audience is always ready to accept her straightforward approach to any subject.

Though Oprah doesn't ask racy questions for their shock value alone, she is often blamed for doing just that. The fact is, if Oprah didn't ask uncomfortable questions, who would? She plays a valuable role in the lives of thousands of women by cutting through the B.S. and getting right to those hardline topics. "I think that for most women," Oprah tells her audience, "it is still difficult, because . . . for a lot of women, who are sitting in small towns and little hamlets and so forth . . . it is very difficult to say, 'I'd like it a little to the left' or 'please me'.'' . . . ''What men don't realize, I think, is that foreplay starts in the morning . . . it starts all day . . . when you come home, how you treat the person, so you can't expect to jump into bed.''

Not one to see only one side of any subject, Oprah shares these thoughts about what men know, and how they learn it. ''Men never really know, unless women tell them. Women,'' she stresses, ''don't know either unless they're told, and there are no courses on it. That's not what they tell you in Health 101. You know . . . ,'' she grins slightly as she smacks her fist into her palm, ''how to actually . . . do it.''

On a show about the relationships between men and women, and the time they spend together, author Shirley Anne Williams responded to the premise that sexual problems caused many relationships to fail. ''Hearing this is very sad to me,'' Williams said, ''because I think that sex is probably the easiest thing to fix in a relationship—once you get over the embarrassment of having to talk about this very intimate problem—because everybody wants to be satisfied.''

Barbara Raskin, another author on this program, told Oprah and the viewers, ''It is . . . hard for women, because sometimes what's happening is that people are talking about 'move to the right'. But there's really a lot more going on. In other words,'' Raskin declares, ''she's thinking, 'Why didn't he help me with the babysitting last week when I needed him?' or 'Why didn't he let me have that new car? Why doesn't he come home on time when I have dinner on the table? Why does he talk to me like that in front of Aunt Fanny?' All of this comes up, in the bedroom . . . she hasn't talked about it all week . . . then he says, 'Just relax and let me love you.' She hasn't talked things out and it interferes with sex,'' Ms. Raskin confidently told Oprah. ''That is exactly when women hurt and don't want to fix a problem in bed.''

Another of Oprah's programming tactics is to have as many women in the audience as she can gather who know how to express themselves as well as (if not more eloquently than) the guest professionals. One young woman confided to Oprah her personal feelings about the available men in her age bracket who approach her for a date. "Hi!" she immediately gushes, not waiting to be asked a particular question, "I'm excited about being thirty years young, I am not excited about the males who are in my age bracket." The woman speaks very quickly without pause. "I'm single, not married, no children." She speaks in such a rush of words it is difficult to follow her. Oprah stands to her right, as though she is a discarded old piece of forgotten furniture, and rolls her eyes. "The males in my age bracket are either married, separated, divorced, paying child support, paying alimony, living with somebody, confused about their sexuality, or have fifteen children by fifteen different women, and it's discouraging to even go out on a date!" The audience chuckles lightly, and tries to hear all that she has to say. The quick-witted, spirited woman continues, "There are guys that say, 'Let's go out on a date.' Right? The date includes them coming over to your home, putting their feet under your table and saying 'serve me'. This is 1987," she demands. "I'm not excited about my sisters . . . who happen to raise some of these males who I have to go out with." Only then, the young woman begins to slow down, trying to sum up her earnest tirade. "Please (to the mothers of these males), could you try something else?"

Oprah asks one of her guests, "Hasn't there always been this feeling that we needed . . . 'him'? Whoever 'him' might be?" Gloria Allred responded, "That is one of the myths, that's one of the fifties fairy tales, that we needed a husband, like we needed a little basic black dress that could take us anywhere. I think they're nice to have," she says matter-of-factly about basic black dresses and men, "but you can get along without them."

Barbara Raskin, a stern-looking thin woman with a

black page-boy haircut, piped in sharply, "The problem is it hasn't just been a myth for many women . . . it was the only way they were going to have that house in the suburbs, the only way they were going to get that new car, and it was the only way that they were going to secure that college education for their kids."

Stephanie Cook, another author who had just written a lengthy article in *GQ* about "what women want," said smartly, "Unfortunate, but that is true. And I'd like to see that changed so that we can have men in our lives and have them as friends and lovers if we want them, but not forced to be there because you don't really have economic options."

During the frequent commercial breaks on her show, Oprah likes to keep moving through the audience while continuing to talk with her guests. She jokes about certain things that were said while the show was on the air. Usually the friendly conversation Oprah carries on during the breaks leads to a more relaxed atmosphere in the heated brightness of the studio. Often she'll grab a bite to eat or have a refreshing drink, hiding them away as the recorded music swells her back on the air. She'll share diet tips and comment on the clothes of the studio audience. When the commercials are over, she steps back into the thick of things and leaps back into form.

When things sometimes become embarrassingly in-depth, Oprah carries her off-camera kidding into the conversation. She likes to use her clowning to ease some of the pressure a certain question might arouse. Some topics are easier dealt with by using humor to lighten the load.

"One of the things I ask women," says Alexandra Penny, is 'what are the three things your husband likes most?' And I'll be amazed to hear that they don't know. One, two, three. They don't know what their husband likes physically."

"Physically," Oprah questions Penny, "You mean . . . sexually?"

"Yes, in making love," Penny says firmly. "Most women can't answer that."

Oprah gestures widely with her arm and looks at the audience. "Can you?" she grins. "Can anyone here answer that question?" The members of the audience exchange sheepish looks with each other, and try to escape Oprah's intent glare and long microphone. Oprah spots an attractive blonde woman who is obviously reluctant to share, even respond on national television, especially with such a personal question. She knew that if she overcame her timidness, and said, "Yes, I know the three physical things my husband likes best," Oprah would then ask her to list them. Oprah thrusts the microphone into the woman's face and waits patiently. The helpless woman smiles nervously and stammers as her face turns three different shades of pale. The audience begins to snicker and Oprah joins them in a rousing belly laugh. The poor woman remains speechless. "I did that," Oprah giggled devilishly, "just to see your facial expression. It was wonderful, thank you!"

In a wink, Oprah returns to the serious business at hand. She turns to tell Alexandra Penny, "But, most women can't."

"Oprah, there's another thing I think is so important that we forget about men. Psychologists call it 'performance anxiety'. I think a lot of women are familiar with this, but I've interviewed so many men and you cannot imagine the anxiety," Ms. Penny explained. "No matter how young, how old, no matter what he says."

One of the strangest shows that Oprah has ever done might have been the time she interviewed a panel of nudists on *A.M. Chicago*. The nudists wanted to extol the virtues of a non-clothed existence and what better way to prove a point than to appear in the nude, which is just what they did. The show caused quite a stir. The audience thought it was the greatest. Oprah, however, had more of a difficult time than she wanted to let on. "We had all these nudists on," Oprah said in *Cosmopolitan*. "I mean, actual naked people," she said, as if the show had happened yesterday. "I pride myself on being real honest, but on this show I was really faking it. I had to act like it was a perfectly normal thing to be interviewing a bunch of naked people and not look." The viewers at home were only shown the nudists from the shoulders up, but Oprah and the studio audience got a considerable eyeful. "I wanted to look into the camera and say, 'My God! There are penises here!' but I couldn't and that made me real nervous."

On a more serious program, Oprah read an introductory letter to her hushed audience as she welcomed the woman who wrote it. "At one time, my three children and I were living in a car. We made a pack of crackers, a loaf of bread, and a can of carrots last for a month. We used to sneak into gas stations to use their soap and their paper towels to bathe with. Then and now I went on a fast not for religious or dieting purposes but to save food."

This is just one example of the real kind of sensationalist topic that Oprah brings to the television screen every weekday. By bringing real people with real problems onto her hour-long show, she keeps the subject matter more in tune with the viewer's life. She also has an undeniably real reserve of experience to use as she questions her viewers, her audience, and herself. She is as real as you and I.

Oprah's executive producer and personal confidante, Debbie DiMaio, expressed her feelings about the qualities that Oprah possesses. "One of Oprah's great gifts is her ability to ask the question that is on the tip of the tongue of everyone watching at home. She's your next-door neighbor. And when you're sitting down watching television with your next-door neighbor, she'll turn to you and say, 'What do you think of that?' I hear this all the time from audiences," DiMaio says fondly. "They come to me and say, 'You know, I feel like I know Oprah Winfrey. I feel like she's a friend of mine. And she always asks what I want to know.' "

"She goes into the show watching it as it's revealed to her, as it is to the studio audience and the viewers at home. In other words," DiMaio explains, "she's not caught in some strict format. If it occurs to Oprah that she wants to ask a question about someone's childhood, then she asks. Everything is very instinctive with her. Usually she's right on the right mark."

Though Oprah tries her best to prove to people that she is a genuine article, she still receives bad press. Charles Whitaker said in *The Saturday Evening Post*, "Oprah's show has obliterated the hold that game shows and Phil Donahue had on daytime ratings; it regularly trounces her competition in head-to-head matchups." Some critics, however, have called her approach "fawning." Some blacks, in particular, charge that Oprah's "touchy-deely" manner toward white members of her predominantly white audience is reminiscent of the stereotypical Southern "mammy."

Oprah is deeply stung by such comments. "I live my life and I do this show to try to raise people's consciousness, to give people a sense of hope in their lives," she says. "So when people write or say negative things about me it really upsets me, because it means that they don't understand me or what my show is about. They've missed it. But I'm convinced that if people who believe that really got to know me, they wouldn't think I was that kind of person."

"Still," Charles Whitaker wrote, "the dominance of *The Oprah Winfrey Show* in the 145 TV markets in which it appears is so complete that local stations on which the show airs clamor to have her promote their news programs in hope that some of the Winfrey magic will rub off on local programming." With that kind of special attention, you might think that Oprah could just slow down and take things on her show a little easier, but that is something that Oprah can't and won't do.

"Oprah does . . . controversial shows," Debbie DiMaio once said, "with guests that have some kind of passion, and emotion, and a story to tell, something that has happened to a person and they've made it through. We call them true-life stories. Usually they're very emotional stories. We always kid her, in some way or another. If we do a show on anything from child abuse to growing up in a broken home, all of that stuff has happened to her. So, unlike the usual blonde, bubble-headed TV talk-show type, she can just turn to the person and say, 'I was there. I can relate to this. Let me tell you how I feel also.' I think that's what makes her special.''

Just like the poor woman who lived in her car with her hungry children, with only the slightest needs met, Oprah has also spend many a hungry time foodless, wishing for some future providence. "I will tell you this," Oprah confided to her silent audience, "I don't have to grocery shop for myself anymore, but there have been many, many, many months that if it wasn't for the 'Food-of-the-Month' club, I would have no food in my refrigerator."

"I don't have any trouble discussing anything from my past," Oprah said once, "including being sexually abused as a child and growing up feeling unloved and looking for love in all the wrong places and just being a frustrated teenager. I think that basically all of us are the same. I had a difficult childhood and other people have a difficult adulthood. I think we are all victimized or feel victimized at some point in our lives, but we have to be responsible for claiming our own victories. So there is nothing that I feel embarrassed or ashamed about, past or present, because I try to live my life so that other people can see the light in me. And that's all anybody can do—be the best they can be."

Another time, Oprah took time out of her busy schedule to say, "I understand that nothing happens to you without your deserving it or creating it in some way for yourself. I believe, from the time you were born, you are empowered with the ability to take responsibility for your life. And to understand that, I'm telling you, makes me joyous. You can allow yourself to be a victim, or you can be the kind of person who understands that you have to take charge. It brings me great joy to know that I have this much control over my life. It's like soaring over the mountains." 'In control' is just what Oprah is when it comes to herself and her career. She has mastered television, film, the stage, and more.

Charles Whitaker said, "The entire country seems to have been swept into a video-love affair with Oprah. Her effusive, off-the-cuff interview style has given a badly needed transfusion to the anemic talk-show format."

"Part of the reason I've been able to do so well . . . is that . . . I am alone," Oprah said about the success of *The Oprah Winfrey Show.* "Up until now I've always been paired with someone else. The thing about working with a co-anchor or a co-host is that it can be stifling, like a bad marriage. Somebody has always got to surrender to the other person. And usually, the person doing the surrendering was me." Oprah worked with many people during her brief stint in broadcasting; co-hosts are a thing of the past for her now. "I knew that I would just bide my time and get good at this—so good that moving to the next place would be easy. That's why I feel very good about where I am right now. I feel I've earned the right to be here."

Although many viewers would love this confident, honest woman to be a guest in their home, not many people would want Oprah to bring along some of the people who have been guests on *The Oprah Winfrey Show.* This would be the case for safety's sake alone. "Would you think it possible in 1987," Oprah asks of her studio audience. "to place a want ad in a magazine for a hired killer?" Well, it happened last year when this ad was placed in *Soldier of Fortune* magazine: "Gun for hire. 37 year old, first professional mercenary, desires job. Viet Nam veteran, discreet, and very private. Bodyguard, other special skills. All jobs considered."

Introducing attorney Doug Norwood, one victim of this bizarre advertisement, Oprah said, "The person who wanted (Doug Norwood) dead answered that ad and paid for a contract killer to do the job. And the killers tried. They knocked down his door and shot him twice in the chest, they bombed his car, and he believes they are still after him. He constantly carries a .357 Magnum, his house is loaded with electronic gear to warn him of intruders, he won't go out at night because he says 'the darkness is a killer's friend'. He refused to fly here to do our show because he thought the place might be bombed. So he drove,'' Oprah said, seemingly without fear of another attack on Norwood's life in the studio. Nothing sobers up a studio audience more than frightening revelations such as these.

"He was not the only victim of the *Soldier of Fortune* magazine gun-for-hire ad,'' she went on. ''The gang of killers who answered that ad left a trail of death and terror across this country.'' The audience began to wriggle uncomfortably. Many of them seemed to be wondering if there was a bomb under their seats, or if another attempt might be made on Norwood's life as Oprah interviewed him (and if he might then pull out his .357 Magnum and spray the audience with gunfire). Fortunately for everyone concerned, this didn't happen.

This type of program is definitely exciting, but it falls into the same 'question and answer' format as the hundreds of other shows that Oprah has done for so long. Oprah, not the type of person to linger in a stagnating format of any kind, recently decided that there was going to be a dramatic change in *The Oprah Winfrey Show*. She and her staff have devised a new format for her already successful program to keep everything fresh and interesting for everyone involved. The show's new appeal will come in the form of definite changes in the way the show will be produced. Oprah wants to keep her show new and different during its second year of national syndication, so she's going out on a limb again—as she's done so many times before.

Oprah and her staff plan to share the excitement of change with her viewers by traveling to cities across the nation to film on location, observing and reporting the timeliest events and interviewing some of the diverse people who live in the United States. Back home in Chicago, the show will have a new set (the familiar set used during her first year, national, is out), and there are plans to finally bring some big name talent to the program. The decision to seek out the Hollywood 'heavies' wasn't all Oprah's, apparently. Debbie DiMaio said recently that the reason they are able to book successful stars like Bill Cosby and Phylicia Rashad on the show was because "They're calling us now."

In a *Star* interview with DiMaio, she told Michael Stinton, "This fall, we are putting our best foot forward, and people will be talking about our shows. More topics, more controversy, more big stars. Bill Cosby is on our schedule," she announced happily, "and we've created a new feature called 'Celebrity Sit Around'."

Says DiMaio, "We want to come up with different combinations that you wouldn't normally see at the same table." The Celebrity Sit Around segment of the new season's shows will feature Oprah talking to two or three celebrities about issues of interest to her viewers. The feature will bring together people whose names are rarely, if ever, mentioned in the same sentence, or who have never met, due to the extreme differences of their varied careers.

The 'on location' programming is still in the planning and development stage at this point, but we will soon see the fruits of DiMaio's labors as she continues to scour the country for the perfect location for the new, revised *Oprah Winfrey Show*. "Because the show is an hour long," DiMaio points out, "the caliber has to be top notch. If we have a celebrity guest, they have to have an interesting personal—as well as professional—side. The whole hour must be entertaining."

With the advent of a newly developed format, a reconstructed set and celebrity bookings, Oprah felt the need to modify her personal appearance as well. There was a change in the air so Oprah decided to change her hair. She met with her creative, personal hairdresser, André Walker, and the two of them came up with a new hair design, with a newer, more glamorous flare. Though the new 'do' looks undoubtedly beautiful, watch for her look to continue to change this season. Oprah plans to keep viewers on their toes by continually switching her hairstyle. She plans to meet with Walker at different times of the year, and experiment with other styles of hair design. "It's a change she wanted," DiMaio said of Oprah's hair, "but it's nothing permanent. There's definitely more to come. A good part of the audience tunes in to see Oprah's clothes; now, maybe, they'll start tuning in to see her new hair."

Oprah's clothes are definitely a central focus to her television personality, though her private wardrobe would strike a chord in anyone's head. An assortment of valuable furs and designer clothes graces the closets of Oprah's $800,000 apartment. Her big, buttoned, bejeweled outfits with striking complementary sashes and bright, colorful bangles have become a trademark of sorts, and her 'style' has spread to all corners of this country. As executive producer DiMaio pointedly remarked, "When Oprah arrived in Chicago, in 1984, she wore big earrings and scarves over her shoulder. Now, every mannequin in every department store window is dressed with earrings and scarves over their shoulder. Even the members of our audience come in with clothes similar to Oprah's," DiMaio proclaimed proudly.

"If you think about it," DiMaio says firmly, "with eleven million viewers watching five days a week, if just one million of these people decide that they like Oprah's (new) look, you've got a fashion trend." People who emulate Oprah's warmth and earthy qualities have begun to show their loyalty by copying her. They have become a part of the fantastic legacy that is Oprah Winfrey.

With all of the new changes in content and style of her award-winning program, Oprah realizes that she'll still be the same Oprah, but she will have to prove that to her audience as well—by bringing herself even closer to the millions of loyal fans who might be turned off by a 'new' Oprah Winfrey. Publicist Alice McGee said about Oprah's

new look, "The new look is a sportier one—more funky
and more casual." Michael Stinton of *Star* commented on
the incredible success of Oprah's daytime pursuits, "Although Donahue had become something of a talk-show
staple to many daytime viewers, Oprah offers something
different—a fresh face, a down-home style of speech, and
the ability to . . . flow right along with those of the
viewers at home."

"As a result," Stinton adds, "legions of fans climbed
aboard with her on her maiden voyage as she tested the
dangerous waters teeming with vigorous competition and
bitter ratings battles."

"But," Stinton says, "she escaped unscathed—aston-
ishingly beating Phil Donahue in the ratings day after
day—and now, the staff has scheduled Oprah to meet with
Phylicia Rashad and Linda Gray in a Celebrity Sit Around
and a third name will be added later."

"I like Phil Donahue," Oprah once said, "but I have to
admit it feels real good to beat him. For the longest time, I
couldn't go about doing my job without people saying,
'Yeah, you're good. But are you as good as Donahue?' "
Without question, Oprah is as good, if not better, than
Donahue.

The excitement of the program's new attractions and
treats will still be overshadowed by Oprah's lovable charm
and conversational capabilities. She'll still become involved
with her audience, and guests, and share her comforting
closeness. The new segments will add variety and a new
vision, but Oprah will remain the same. Obviously thrilled
with the upcoming changes, Debbie DiMaio told Michael
Stinton, "Oprah will travel four times a year to either New
York or Los Angeles, and have lunch with three celebrities."

"They'll eat and talk for three hours and then we'll put
the best stuff together for an hour show. It's a great idea
because the celebrities will be seen in a different light. It's
a chance for them to really let their hair down and talk
openly. That's when they really open up." With those
benefits aside, for a woman who is doing her best to lose

some of the weight that plagues her, it is an ironic twist of fate that puts Oprah in the precarious position of being paid to eat on television.

"You'll find that the show will take to the road a lot more often this year," Debbie DiMaio says promisingly. "It's a nice backdrop and change of scenery, rather than doing all of the shows from the studio. We'll be looking for controversy and people with something (important) to say."

DiMaio, who is Oprah's personal friend, as well as her professional companion, swells with exuberance when talking about Oprah. She loves to tell people what's going on with her. "There is a great power in the medium of television, and with that we can make positive changes in people's lives. You'll continue to be entertained, if not by the guests, then always by Oprah."

Oprah Winfrey, since the beginning of her talk-show career, has always strived to keep her approach fresh and inviting. The way she takes control on her program, and turns it toward a directiion of her own, wasn't always the way she was supposed to do the show. Her large amount of control came to her the time she had Tom Selleck on her program. When faced with a mostly preplanned script with which to interview Selleck (a long-time favorite of Oprah's), she requested that she be allowed to throw away the script and do the interview off the cuff. Permission was granted and the show worked well. Oprah had plenty to talk about with her handsome guest. She was all business with him, asking crucial, intelligent questions like, "Did you know your eyes are the color of a crystal blue sea?"

Later Oprah discussed her feelings with the production managers and staff. She was dissatisfied with the scripted shows and had already felt the freedom of a non-scripted one. "It just doesn't work for me," she said. "It throws me totally off balance. How can I ask a question if I already know the answer? I look like I'm faking it." The mutual decision was that Oprah would go scriptless and be allowed the freedom to do just what she does best: talk to people.

From that point on, the staff would provide Oprah with a packet of informational material about the guests which she would study. Then, when the time came to sit down and talk to the people, she would ask those questions that, she felt, needed to be asked. She could make up her own mind as to where to lead the talk or questioning, and she could now interject whatever thoughts or feelings she might have. Oprah's no-nonsense type of program consistently beats shows like Donahue because of her ability and responsibility to be as informal or spontaneous as she sees fit.

The Donahue/Winfrey comparisons have been the subject of many conversations about Oprah Winfrey. Though there is a slight similarity in content (they both ask questions), her staunchest supporters realize the significance of their differences. There was a time, however, when Oprah worried that the two programs may be too parallel in operation. She once said, "I used to watch him (Phil Donahue) all the time. I'd tape Donahue (which aired at the same time as her show)." Oprah found herself needing to watch less Donahue tapes, though, when she found that she and Phil Donahue shared a few mannerisms. "There was a point when I noticed I was doing the same thing with the microphone that he does and I said, 'Phil does that.' One day, on the air, I said, 'Hey, would you help me out here?' " (This, as you probably know, is one of Mr. Donahue's often-used lines.) "And then I said," Oprah recalls, "Oh boy! I've been watching too much Phil! I have the greatest respect for him, though," Oprah reaffirms. "I learned how to do what I do because of him."

Oprah Winfrey may seem like the talk-show format's greatest host, and that she is so at home there that she'll never leave it, but she is much more. She is a multitalented performer. Gifted with the ease of enactment and character absorption, Oprah weaves her own personality into the fictional personalities in her films.

Oprah learned much about her thespian abilities while a student at Tennessee State University's drama department. It was here that she began her stagecraft and learned to hone her abilities. While studying at T.S.U., Oprah would perform one-woman dramatic readings, often accompanied by a group of girls her age who would bring her words to full life with gospel songs and rousing rhythms, music, and song. She also performed outside of the university, made church appearances, and attended out-of-town competitive conferences. She was (and still is) the center of attention wherever she went. The group she performed in, Sweet Honey in the Rock, performed to many an appreciative audience in crowded church halls and other social gatherings. People just couldn't take their eyes off of her, and her endearing charm led them through a swirl of emotions as she gave her dramatic readings. Her family, friends, churchmates, and classmates watched as Oprah gained her early experience in the theater.

Oprah's former mentor/drama instructor at Tennessee State University, Dr. William Cox II, told me that Oprah's impact on the students in his department's classes has been considerable. With Oprah to use as an example of the achievements that are possible to those who perservere, ''Nothing can be more inspiring to a Black student than to have an internationally known Black person to use as a model.''

Oprah's first major motion picture project, *The Color Purple* (Oprah's favorite color), took place near Nashville, so naturally the students from Tennessee State University, in Nashville, came in droves to see it. Nashville wasn't the only place where *The Color Purple* was successful. The film won numerous awards and was held over in theaters across the country and beyond.

Dr. Cox acknowledges that he watches Oprah's television show now and then. He told me, ''I watch Ms. Winfrey's show occasionally. It is viewed here (Nashville) at 4 P.M. C.S.T. daily. When we are in production, my responsibilities take me away from the tube,'' he admits.

But he will always remember Oprah as a stage actor, or even a movie star, before he thinks of her as a talk-show host. He just has too many memories of Oprah doing serious material. In *Oprah!* by Robert Waldron, Dr. Cox revealed, "I get concerned that no one knows about her experience at T.S.U. in the theater. I think that most people get the idea that her first major acting move was in *The Color Purple*. But Oprah did a great deal of theater within our department," Dr. Cox recalled. He also remembers Oprah's gospel and theatrical group. "She had a young group that called themselves Sweet Honey in the Rock. I think every Sunday they were booked in a church with their program, with dramatic readings from *God's Trombones* by James Johnson. It was a one-woman drama with a group of religious singers backing her up. I think she knew every bit of poetry in *God's Trombones*. I never see anything like this in print," said Oprah's former drama coach. "It bothers me."

Oprah's childhood and her college days weren't all peaches and cream, though. Her father kept her under a tight rein; she was guilt-ridden from a series of sexual abuses she endured as a child. She survived beatings at the hand of her cruel grandmother, poverty, juvenile delinquency, and constant ridicule from certain college classmates for not being an outspoken activist for the Black movement. She didn't have an afro, she didn't grease her hair, and she didn't always agree with some of her classmates' political motivitations.

"Today," Charles Whitaker said in *The Saturday Evening Post*, "Oprah Winfrey, 33 (she'll turn a young 34 in January 1988), is a bona-fide phenomenon and media darling. She has been featured on magazine covers (like *The Saturday Evening Post*) and profiles on television. Her life story has been retold in so many periodicals that even she is beginning to wonder if it doesn't sound like a cliché."

"Actually, the Oprah Winfrey story is part Horatio Alger, part Booker T. Washington, and part Cinderella. Born in Mississippi, she was first reared by her mother, and when she became too precocious to handle, in Nashville by her father and stepmother. Hers was a typically poor-to-working-class childhood she describes as "not much different from anybody else's who grew up in the black experience during the time that I grew up."

"During her sophomore year at T.S.U.," Mr. Whitaker wrote, "she was recruited by a local TV station to become a reporter. She has spent virtually all of her adult life in front of the camera. After graduation from college, she moved to Baltimore to become the news anchor at WJZ-TV, the ABC affiliate there. Then, in 1984, it was on WLS-TV in Chicago, where she transformed the failing *A.M. Chicago* show into the giant killer that toppled the venerable Donahue."

Today she drives a brand-spanking-new Jaguar Xj-S, a symbol of her triumph over seemingly unsurmountable odds. She lives in an expensive apartment on the high side of town; she wears thousand-dollar outfits and wears hundred-dollar shoes (though she has pairs that cost more). Yet she hasn't turned her back on the people who haven't yet reached their pinnacle, as she has.

It was an abrupt leap for Oprah, though. She told *Forbes* that "she made her first million only last year, when King World sold her program nationally." Her syndicate, King World, distributes television shows like *Tic Tac Dough, Joker's Wild, Jeopardy,* and the ever popular *Wheel of Fortune.* When the executives saw the impact Oprah had on her Chicago program, they realized her potential and that of her show. They offered an immediate sample of their intentions by delivering a check to Oprah's boss for one million dollars. King World is taking *The Oprah Winfrey Show* for a five year trial run. The show has already earned King World hundreds of millions of dollars, and the best is yet to come.

part two—OW!

Oprah Winfrey is one star sitting in the lap of luxury who doesn't forget her past. She may drive a new Jaguar, but she remembers when she couldn't afford to make a phone call. She stretches out in her full-size marble bath, with gold animal-shaped fixtures, and remembers her less-than-clean early childhood when she didn't have shoes and ran through the barnyard with no other children to play with. "There was an outhouse," Oprah said to Norman King in *Good Housekeeping*, "in the back, and a well about a hundred yards from the house."

Oprah's grandmother, who had full charge of her, was often a cruel and thoughtless woman. She used to whip Oprah whenever she could, with switches of varying length. "I used to get whipped every day," she remembered. "I was always getting into trouble and I always thought I could get away with it. But I am what I am because of my grandmother. My strength, my sense of reasoning . . . all of that was set by the time I was six years old. I basically am no different now than I was when I was six." Except that now she can enjoy the success of her achievements.

"This morning as I sat in my marble tub," she said to Charles Whitaker, "surrounded by bubbles, with the water

21

pouring from the golden-swan faucet, I thought, as I opened my box of apple-cinnamon soap, 'Is this it? Is this what being a celebrity is all about?' It's interesting because I don't feel any different. My ability to acquire things has changed, but *I* don't feel any different. So I keep saying to myself, 'Well, I guess I'm not a star yet, because I don't feel like one.' " Her newly redecorated marble-floored condominium is filled with custom-made furniture and decorated in purple and cream. She doesn't keep all of her wealth to herself, though. Oprah's charitable donations exceed hundreds of thousands of dollars, not including her valuable time; she spends hundreds of hours with anti-drug organizations, church groups, and youth organizations. Oprah also has a habit of giving friends and associates expensive and lavish gifts. Charles Whitaker offers this example. "Two Christmases ago, when the seven members of her staff were denied raises by station bosses, Oprah gave each staffer $10,000 in cash stuffed inside rolls of toilet paper." "It was great," she says. "Everyone wept and had a wonderful time. It feels good to be able to do things like that with no strings attached, just because I can."

She isn't an easy touch, though. "I do not have people around me who want anything from me other than my friendship and my emotional support. I have the most difficult time giving things to people who I think want them. The minute I get asked for anything, my red flag goes up."

Oprah isn't afraid that she might lose all that she has striven to acquire. She is confident in her abilities, and she believes that there are more great things in store for her in the future. Oprah says that she has recently been undergoing a 'spiritual evolution' that has allowed her to "press to the mark of the high calling, as Paul said." She doesn't consider her new feelings a reawakening of her spiritual beliefs. "It's not being born again, it's an evolution, a realization of how life works—meaning that God is the center of the universe. Once you understand that, it's all really very simple." If Oprah ever turned to an evangelical calling, she would already have a substantial following.

Oprah says that she often reads her Bible and gets down on her knees to pray, each and every day. "I remember when I was little and my grandmother first taught me to pray. She said, 'As long as you have the power to bow your head and bend your knees, you do it and God will hear you better.' I have not been able to get that out of my brain," she recalls.

With God, and Stedman Graham on her side, Oprah has a lot to look forward to. The 6-foot, 6-inch former European basketball player and male model is a constant companion to Ms. Winfrey. They enjoy spending time with each other and sharing intimate thoughts. The two are often seen walking briskly together as they cavort on the cool streets of Chicago. Compared to her former male/female relationships, her latest is a romantic advanture. There were times when Oprah let herself lose some of her dignity and live in precarious situations. "The relationships I had were totally detrimental. I was a doormat. But the thing about it is you realize that there is a doormat overload out there because everybody's been one. Now I say, 'I will never give up my power to another person.' "

It's sometimes difficult to imagine that someone as busy as Oprah still finds time to spend with family and friends, but she takes so much pleasure in their company that she makes the time to be with them. She spent her last Thanksgiving in her old hometown, Nashville, with her father, Vernon Winfrey. The Winfreys made their holiday complete by visiting some of her youthful haunts.

"We went to Mississippi together," Vernon Winfrey told Norman King. "She went by the old church where she gave her first speech and she visited all the old folk." Still the same Southern-bred woman, Oprah did her best to remind herself of what it was like to live there by doing what she could to help those she met. "She saw this one elderly lady," Mr. Winfrey remembered fondly, "and wanted to know if she wanted her to bring in any firewood. She's still level-headed. Her feet are still on the ground.''

Oprah's pursuit of interesting people and fascinating stories took her to Midland, Texas recently, where she interviewed Jessica McLure, the little girl who, by becoming trapped in a deep well and being saved in a dramatic full-scale rescue undertaking, became 'America's little miracle'. Oprah talked with the girl and her lucky mother in an emotionally charged interview.

Still, there are some people who see every humanitarian thing she does in the wrong way. Those who think that Oprah is leeching the victimized, or exploiting the deprived, tend to make fun of her endeavors, without seeming to care how their statements affect her. David Letterman mentioned that Oprah had announced she was going to Midland for the interview with Jessica McLure on his program, *Late Night* (10/27/87). Then he went into a cruel tirade, mocking Oprah, her clothes, her recent weight loss (''I like the old Oprah better,'' Letterman kept saying throughout the show). He even made fun of her former weight, after claiming he preferred her that way, and joked, ''I guess we don't have to worry about Oprah falling down the well.'' He was obviously a little upset with Oprah's sudden acceptance by the American public and in a typically jealous fashion, he mocked her over and over. ''She looks great,'' Letterman told his audience. But he kept returning to her recent weight loss, saying that Oprah now ''looks just like Diana Ross.'' ''I don't want to spend the rest of my life,'' Letterman said roughly, ''kissing up to this woman.'' Then he blurted out, ''Haven't we seen enough shoulder pads? And they're getting bigger!'' he joked.

Maybe Mr. Letterman is worried that *The Oprah Winfrey Show* might be rescheduled against his time slot, and thus wreck his ratings like she's done to so many other programs. One must take the things David Letterman says with a grain of salt. His mischievous temperament has a good-natured side to it; in reality, he's not out to hurt anyone with his offhand comments. I laughed through the whole Oprah bit, because this just shows how far Oprah's reputation has spread. Whether you like her or not, chances are, if you own a television, you know who she is.

Oprah is not totally immune to the kind of jokes that people make about her. "It bothers me when we are accused of being sensational and exploitative," Oprah said of her challengers. "We are a caring group of people." Oprah really does care and she takes a lot of pressure for doing the kinds of stories that she does, because they truly effect her. She would often break into tears, as a news reporter. She still does when confronted by any touching topic, and she always will be effected, emotionally. She is a sensitive and caring person, doing her best to bring understanding and compassion to her millions of viewers.

Oprah never falters in her constant desire to do bigger and better things with her life. Who could have imagined that the petite girl with a homemade dress and bare, dirty feet would rise from the dust of her grandmother's farm and do the many great things that Oprah has done. A nonstop performer, she had barely completed her second motion picture, *Native Son*, when she immediately began working on her latest film, *The Women of Brewster Place*. She also has an ABC situation comedy in the works in which she plans to star. The show is about a black female talk-show host and her way of life. She will play the woman, with herself as a model. The program will air weekly, in a half-hour format, and will bring Oprah's humorous side to light. Films, television comedies, personal appearances, and a dazzling new talk-show format will ensure Oprah's future popularity and financial prosperity.

"I try to move with the flow of life," Oprah once said of her future plans, "and not dictate what life should be for me, but just let it flow. So, there may be a husband and there may be children. There may not. I will celebrate either course that my life hands me." "Some people don't know how to take me sometimes. But I'm honest. I really am. I do just what I feel and hope it works."

2

Young Miss Winfrey—
The Little Speaker

"Flaming youth has become a flaming question. And youth comes to us wanting to know what we may propose to do about a society that hurts so many of them."

—FRANKLIN D. ROOSEVELT

Oprah Gail Winfrey was born in Kosciusko, Mississippi, on January 29, 1954. Born on her maternal grandmother's isolated farm, where her parents, Vernon Winfrey and Vernita Lee, lived, she came into the world with the assistance of local midwives.

Being born on the farm was most certainly due to convenience. Money matters aside, other factors superseded a hospital birth. First of all, in 1954, segregated hospitals were the norm; in fact, that year the Department of Health, Education and Welfare reaffirmed its policy of giving funds to segregated hospitals. It just didn't make sense to travel twenty to seventy miles to have a baby in a "Negro" hospital. In addition, most forms of travel were expensive and race-restricted at that.

One midwife, in charge of writing out Oprah's birth

certificate, misspelled her intended name, 'Orpah' (after the Biblical Orpah, Ruth's sister). Thus a star was named.

Oprah's parents had never married and soon went separate ways, leaving Oprah with her strict grandmotheer. By the tender age of 2½, Oprah's grandmother had taught her to read. According to *Current Biography* (March 1987), she had already "blossomed as a public speaker at the age of two, when she addressed the congregation of a rural church on the topic of 'Jesus rose on Easter Day'."

Oprah's free time was spent mostly with the farm animals, chickens and cows, which she fed and kept. She also spend numerous hours in the company of another close friend, a corncob doll. This may sound pleasant, but the rigors and chores of farm life were exhausting and tough for a little girl. Oprah's grandmother often forced her to tend the animals. She even beat and whipped Oprah to be sure she kept up with her chores.

As far as Oprah's elementary education was concerned, "When she was enrolled in kindergarten, she promptly wrote a note that pointed out in no uncertain terms that she belonged in the first grade, and her astonished teacher had her promoted. After completing that academic year, she skipped directly to the third grade" (*Current Biography*).

Oprah continued her holiday and church speeches, but her life changed when she was sent to live with her mother and two half-brothers at the age of six. Her mother, Vernita Lee, lived in the ghetto of Milwaukee. She struggled to supplement her welfare payments by working as a maid. Money was scarce and friendly barnyard animals even rarer. Oprah didn't have a dog or other domesticated pets. Instead, she utilized what animals were available in her lowly surroundings: cockroaches. Oprah corraled her little pals into old jars and gave them names such as "Melinda" and "Sandy."

Because of her elocutionary talents, Oprah Winfrey was invited again and again to speak at church events and black social organizations. These recitations led some to call her "the little speaker." During a brief visit to Nashville,

Oprah earned $500 for a speech she gave at her father's church. After her speech, Miss Winfrey announced that for a living she wanted to be "paid to talk."

Upon returning to Milwaukee, Oprah found her mother still struggling to support the family with a meager $50 a month domestic's salary and whatever welfare provided. In her mother's absence, Oprah fell prey to numerous acts of sexual use and abuse by "trusted friends." She was even raped by her mother's boyfriend.

The abuse started when Oprah was nine and continued until she left her mother to live with her father. Each sexual attack left Oprah feeling confused and guilty. She was threatened and bribed into silence by her attackers. Her half-brother took Oprah to the zoo and bought her ice cream so she wouldn't tell anyone of his hideous offenses. Oprah, deeply hurt, didn't speak of these crimes against her until she talked with a woman who had also been abused as a child. This took place during one of Oprah's television shows, many years later.

During the taping of the fateful show, Oprah, the woman she was talking to, and the studio audience shared her personal tragedy as she embraced the truth and, for the first time, publicly admitted her abuse. Oprah received hundreds of sympathetic calls from women who had been similarly abused as children. Many a common tear was shed in this emotional hour.

In an interview with Joan Barthel of *Ms. Magazine* (August 1986), Oprah spoke of these trying times, saying that "it happened at my own house by different people— this man, that cousin." Oprah tries to downplay the horrible events, though they seem to stick with her like scars on skin. "I don't like making a big deal out of it. I remember blaming myself for it, thinking something must be wrong with me."

Due to this increasingly sordid home life, Oprah began to indulge in acts of delinquency. Once, her mother refused to buy Oprah a new set of eyeglasses (her old pair was 'butterfly-framed' and not at all the fashion with her peers at the 'all white school' she was bused to), so she faked a dramatic robbery. Oprah smashed her fashionless glasses and ransacked her mother's home. When questioned, she feigned amnesia.

Another time, Oprah saw singer Aretha Franklin exiting an expensive limousine. She approached the famous lady and told such a convincing tale of abandonment that Ms. Franklin gave her one hundred dollars to help Oprah "get home to Ohio." Oprah then rented a room in a Milwaukee hotel with the money. When the cash ran out, she returned home in the company of a minister. The stint didn't go over well with Vernita Lee, who took Oprah to the local detention center for delinquents.

The Winfrey providence was with Oprah as always. No beds or rooms were available in the detention center so Oprah was not accepted. At a loss for professional experience and assistance, Vernita Lee contacted Vernon Winfrey and asked that he and his wife take charge of Oprah.

"The past has made me stronger," Oprah told Thomas Morgan in a *New York Times* article (March 4, 1986). "Not getting the attention from my mother made me seek it in other places," she said, still blaming herself, "the wrong places, until my father came and got me from my mother in Milwaukee and took me to Nashville where he lived. His discipline channeled my need for love and attention into a new direction."

A new direction indeed. Oprah's father was even more strict than her grandmother had been. Vernon and his wife, Velma, applied various methods of obedience and ethical training. They first insisted that Oprah learn a new word each day, with the promise of no dinner if she faltered. She was also to write a book report every week. Quite a bit for a young girl struggling with a new school, a new home structure, and the memories of an abusive and very personal past.

Vernon and Velma's strict encouragement turned out to be a boon, though, and Oprah progressively prospered in and out of her new scholastic upbringing. "My father saved my life," Oprah said to Randy Banner of the *New York Daily News* (September 7, 1986).

Vernon Winfrey was a barber. He was also on the Nashville City Council. He was a strict father yet a compassionate man. Mr. Winfrey supplied Oprah with books, clothes, personal guidance, and never refused to talk with her about her needs and problems. Sometimes he would even stay up late into the night to do so.

In high school Oprah joined the drama club, was an honor student, and held a high position in the student body council, already preparing for her future acting and oratory events. She won an Elks Club oratorical contest which provided a full scholarship to Tennessee State University (T.S.U.). At sixteen this was quite an accomplishment, but still a far cry from her acting and humanitarian accomplishments of today.

At T.S.U. Oprah worked toward her Bachelor of Science degree in drama and speech. While attending the university, she was a news reporter for the black radio station WVOL, thus beginning her career as a broadcaster.

Oprah's work for WVOL came about while she was still in high school. She entered a contest the station sponsored, won, and was crowned Miss Fire Prevention. Along with this title and a beautiful Longenes watch, WVOL hired Oprah as their news anchor. Up until a few months before her high school graduation, she left for work as soon as classes ended to become the voice of WVOL News, every hour on the hour.

Concerning her Miss Fire Prevention award, Oprah said to Audrey Edwards (*Essence,* October 1986), "I know it's not a biggie, but I was the only black—the first black—to win the darned thing. I went on from there and entered the Miss Black Nashville contest, because I'd gotten all this publicity for being the first black to win the Miss Fire Prevention contest."

Oprah was voted Miss Black Nashville in 1971 and entered the Miss Black Tennessee pageant. "I didn't expect to win, nor did anybody else expect me to," Oprah told Ms. Edwards, "because there were all these vanillas (light-skinned girls) and here I was a fudge child. And Lord, were they upset, and I was for them, really I was. I said, 'Beats me girls, I'm as shocked as you are. I don't know how I won either.' "

The reasons Oprah was a beauty pageant winner then are the same reasons she is such a popular star today. "I had marvelous poise and talent and could handle any question, and I would always win on the talent part, which was usually a dramatic reading. I could—I still can—hold my own easily. Ask me anything, and my policy has always been to be honest, to tell the truth. Don't try to think of something to say, just say whatever is the truth."

When talking to Chris Anderson, Oprah spoke of her future as a broadcaster. "When the judges asked me what I wanted to do with my life, I was going to say, 'become a fourth grade teacher', but I had seen Barbara Walters that morning on the *Today Show,* and it just popped into my head to say I wanted to be a journalist."

With all this exposure and attention, it was only a matter of time before someone would spot her talents and set her career-ball rolling. That 'someone' was the local CBS affiliate, WTVF-TV, Nashville. After refusing numerous job offers from WTVF, Oprah finally accepted a position at the insistence of her speech teacher. This instructor simply mentioned that job offers from companies like CBS were the reason most people attended college. A sound reasoning, that.

Oprah was the first black woman, in fact the first woman, to ever hold a position as co-anchor on the evening news in Nashville. "Sure I was token," Oprah told Judy Markey of *Cosmopolitan* (September 1986), "but honey, I was one happy token."

In an interview with Gary Ballard (*Drama-Logue,* March 1986), Oprah spoke of her father's preoccupation with disciplinary teachings, saying that she was "the only news anchor in the country who had to be home by midnight." Although she had secured a job that paid $15,000 per year while she was only a junior in college, Oprah was, as ever, under Daddy's thumb.

In 1976 Oprah Winfrey graduated from Tennessee State University with a Bachelor of Science degree. She also graduated from living with Vernon Winfrey. Oprah was more than happy to leap into a new position as reporter and co-anchor for WJZ-TV, the ABC affiliate in Baltimore. When the offer came, it was time for Oprah to leave for Baltimore; Vernon and Velma Winfrey stayed behind.

3

A'nt I a Woman?

A'nt I a Woman?

—SOJOURNER TRUTH

Ain't it somethin'?

—OPRAH WINFREY

In the year of America's Bicentennial, Oprah left the comforts and security of her father's Nashville home. She was on her way to an enlightening new job with WJZ-TV in stately Baltimore, Maryland. Her new career as a big city tele-journalist seemed to be bountiful and challenging. And challenging it was.

Even though Oprah was fresh out of college, she was far from being green in the area of professional broadcasting. However, she still carried with her an innocence, which was about to be tested to the limits by some of her most trying and difficult times, as a news reporter and co-anchor for the evening news on WJZ-TV, Baltimore.

A news reporter must keep all signs of personal feelings

33

and prejudice under a tight veil of emotionless stability. Only hard-nosed fact, mixed with a subject of common interest, reaches the news-ready viewer's waiting eye. Sometimes a good news reporter must fight off deeply felt emotion and turn a cold shoulder to human tragedy in order to present a professional report.

While reading the news to her six o'clock audience, Oprah often had to fight back her own emotions so as to dish out the main course news. In the face of pain, she swallowed her empathy and gave hard-line stories a stern, almost emotionless delivery.

When confronted with having to cover a truly tragic story, one of a distraught mother whose little children had died in a fiery blaze, Oprah had to "fight back the tears" and interview the woman, asking her to reveal her feelings of recent personal loss. Oprah almost didn't do it, as few of us could. But she was faced with the possibility of losing her job (which she actually did later on) if she did not return, as ordered, to the site of the inferno and continue the interview with the poor woman who had lost her house and children. Not acquiescing completely to her boss's whims, Oprah apologized to the woman, and to her viewers, while she introduced the piece live on the air.

These and other such events led Oprah to the realization that news was not her forté. In *Good Housekeeping* (August 1986), she said, "I'd have to fight back the tears if a story was too sad. I just didn't have the detachment." Oprah stressed to Joan Barthel that she had been "hating every minute of it."

Oprah's problems didn't end with her emotional attachment. The assistant news director for WJZ-TV wasn't happy with her looks either. It was one thing to have a black woman news anchor, yet another thing entirely to have a black woman news anchor who *looks* black.

Oprah's Nashville style of journalism differed from what the heads of WJZ-TV had in mind. She often set aside her lines and script until the last minute in order to keep the stories *fresh*. The last thing Oprah wanted was to be bored with her presentation. Sadly (in the short run), the Oprah Winfrey/Jerry Turner team didn't work out and Oprah was dismissed from her job by Al Sanders.

After losing her anchor position because of her ethnic appearance, Oprah tried to comply with the assistant news director's plan to change her into his ideal of a perfect-looking anchor. In his view, Oprah would look better as a "Puerto Rican." She agreed to fly to New York for a complete make-over and speech lessons. Why the assistant news director of WJZ-TV didn't try to make Oprah look white is a matter of speculation, but in any case the attempted beautification was fruitless. "Your hair's too thick, your nose is too wide, and your chin's too big," Oprah recounted to Cheryl Lavin of her news director's opinionated statements (*Chicago Tribune*, September 19, 1985).

Later in New York, the beauticians set to making-over Oprah Winfrey. They went a little wild with their over-indulging attempts though, and at best, their efforts were for the worst. A flubbed-up permanent left her totally and completely bald. This was not quite what the assistant news director had in mind, no doubt, but that's the way it was. It's a good thing he hadn't demanded she try cosmetic surgery.

"You learn a lot about yourself," she told Joan Barthel, "when you're bald" (*Ms.*, August 1986). "I felt the (perm) lotion burning my skull, and I kept saying, 'Excuse me, this is beginning to burn a little.' They kept saying, 'Oh just a few more minutes.' " Within a week, every hair had crisply fallen out.

"If you're black and walk into a place where every-body's speaking French, *run* in the opposite direction," Oprah cautioned Chris Anderson in *Good Housekeeping* (August 1986). "There were no wigs big enough for my head—it's 24½ inches around—so I had to walk around wearing scarves for months. I was devastated, and had to find some way to get back my self-esteem. Which is hard when you're a black, bald, out-of-work anchorwoman."

Out of a job and embarrassingly bald, Oprah turned inward toward a soul-searching self-discovery. She was demoted to doing short cut-ins on the ABC network's *Good Morning America*, and was an Instant Eye reporter in WJZ's mobile unit. Baltimore just wasn't treating her right. Oprah longed to move forward.

During this odd but trying time, Oprah was dating reporter Lloyd Kramer. Was Lloyd frightened of Oprah's new space age looks? No; in fact Oprah's new 'do' caused the two to experience a romantic surge of affection for one another. Oprah still views her relationship with Lloyd Kramer fondly.

In 1977, WJZ-TV 'risked' giving Oprah another chance. This time they had her work as a co-anchor on a talk show, *Baltimore Is Talking*, after starting her out by doing local updates and cut-ins on ABC's *Good Morning America*. On this somewhat more casual show Oprah was able to use her considerable charm and personality, a welcome change from the demands of her previous duties. For Oprah it was like an overdue breath of fresh mountain air. This was her chance to really begin to shine as a TV personality. She was now able to be personable and candid with her audience and guests. As she reported to Chris Anderson, ''The minute the first show was over, I thought 'Thank God. I've found what I was meant to do.' It's like breathing to me.''

For the next seven years, Oprah and her co-anchor Richard Sher interviewed some of the most bizarre and interesting guests available. The two made a rating-breaking pair as they attacked every imaginable topic and guest. The viewing audience continued to choose *Baltimore Is Talking* over other shows airing in the same time slot. The ratings for the show even surpassed those of Phil Donahue. This wasn't the last time Oprah Winfrey made a puddle of Phil Donahue's ratings, as you'll see later. Oprah Winfrey is a name Mr. Donahue most probably will never fail to remember.

Baltimore had made a new friend. In no time at all, Oprah was the local queen of daytime Baltimore.

With the opportunity to show her intimate side and candid conversation, and the ability to draw a story out of a guest like a magician smoothly unfolding a snow-white dove, Oprah caught the attention of Dennis Swanson, the general manager of television station WLS, an ABC affiliate in Chicago. Her talents were so apparent to Mr. Swanson, and so appealing were her impressive Baltimore ratings, that he hired not just Oprah but her Baltimore produce Debbie DiMaio as well.

Mr. Swanson needed someone like Oprah for WLS's lackluster talk show, *A.M. Chicago*, a failing, and consistently bad, morning show. Oprah went where many others had failed, and turned the show into something more to her liking. Originally the program was geared to the docile housewife whose central interests concerned the texture of makeup and creating the perfect casserole. Since eating a casserole interested Oprah much more than talking about one, she turned *A.M. Chicago* into an upbeat issue-oriented show with a biting wit and shared insights. Oprah chucked out the pudding and began to cut the meat.

A.M. Chicago gained a well-earned reputation for entertaining subjects which were topical and controversial. Due to the city's reputation for racial polarization, even to the point of being picketed outside of the studio, Oprah was pleased to find a loyal and comfortable following. She was welcomed into Chicago's heart because of the consistent quality of her shows, not because of her looks. WJZ-TV in Baltimore learned a lesson, we must hope, for the acceptance of quality must always come before an incomplete understanding of what an audience will accept as professional—black or white, fat or thin.

In a few short weeks *A.M. Chicago* leapt over Donahue's ratings, even though he had dominated the local talk show ratings for more than sixteen seasons. Oprah Winfrey was now Chicago's new favorite. She had them by their hearts and no one was complaining but Mr. Donahue. By September 1985, Oprah's ratings were well above anything Chicago had to offer. The *A.M. Chicago* show was changed to the now famous *Oprah Winfrey Show*.

Crediting Phil Donahue with making possible new talk show formats, which "paved the way" for the type of show for which she became famous, Oprah acknowledges his contribution to quality programming. This proved that daytime TV audiences wanted more than programmed pap, that they enjoyed more than mascara and ladies underwear. Instead, they demanded to learn about the new views and activities of the women and men of today. Having finally found her métier, Oprah Winfrey became a happy talk show gazelle, bounding through the vast pastures of daytime television, with no lions in sight.

During an interview with actor Tom Selleck, on *The Oprah Winfrey Show*, Oprah turned the show even further to her liking by asking the station's management if she could throw out the cue cards and interview the actor just as she would a friend. They abandoned the written script and adlibbed the entire show. This advancement led Alan Richman of *People* magazine to describe her as "a mind as quick as any in television, yes, Carson and Letterman included."

4

Love and Life

*Behold, I do not give lectures or a little charity,
when I give I give myself.*

—WALT WHITMAN

Before going on to Oprah's television and motion picture achievements, I'd like to slow down for a bit and get into some of her more personal pursuits. It might seem as though our favorite super-stars lead lives rich in carefree extravagance, and at times we might forget that those we idolize have personal lives.

In Oprah Winfrey's life, there have been, and there will continue to be, personal, sometimes very private, trying times. The problems you and I must face and deal with are not altogether different than those we idolize must also endure. Anxiety, love, social acceptance, and self-satisfaction are as much a part of Oprah Winfrey's life as they are of ours. As human beings, we are all too aware of our own problems; it may help us to think that persons we emulate are above the day-to-day antagonisms which we continually endure. Well, they're human too. Naturally, Oprah has had some hard times, like we all do. But it's what we do with these experiences that enrich our understanding of the lives we lead.

One of the running themes in Oprah's conversations with her audience is that of her weight. In case you haven't noticed, Oprah weighs around 190 pounds, though lately she's been trying to slim down. Some people complain about her weight, saying that a TV host should be slim, trim, and pretty. Others like Oprah just the way she is. They begin to worry that if she should lose her extra weight, she might not come across as warm and endearing as she does now. They seem to think that a skinny Oprah just wouldn't have the same personality that they've come to love. When this subject comes up, Oprah likes to quip, "Honey, it ain't in my thighs." Since this comes up all too often, she changes the sayings to keep her responses fresh, like inserting "bottom" for thighs.

Being Oprah Winfrey, she must have an honest self-image. When talking about her body, Oprah uses the same honest approach that she uses when discussing any other topic. In *Essence*, she told Audrey Edwards, "I am not blonde and I am not thin." Though she accepts her size, she's not always pleased with it. She knows the depths of her limitations and the possibilities of her achievements.

The intense pressures of running a nationally syndicated talk show today are as real to Oprah Winfrey now as they were in her early days when she made her move from Baltimore to Chicago. She told Audrey Edwards, "Everybody kept telling me that it was going to be impossible to succeed because I was going into Phil Donahue's hometown . . . So, you know, I'd eat. I'd eat out of the nervousness of it all . . . and then people were saying 'There are going to be pickets outside your door.' "

After Oprah's bout with the New York beauticians, she turned to food for solace. The extra weight began then and continues to this day. Now, however, she turns to another comfort these days, namely Stedman Graham. Recently, she has even taken to doing a little jogging, to impress her new-found love, though she still retains much of her weight. Oprah told Audrey Edwards that she took up jogging "because Steds has such an incredible body." True, Graham, a former model, stands almost a foot taller than Oprah and is as healthy as they come.

Some people are almost to the point of being rude when confronting Oprah Winfrey's plentiful size. Stephanie Mansfield, while delivering an endearing description of Oprah, began her article in the *Washington Post* by calling her "Fat City" and continued, "She's Big. Really Big. If she gets any bigger, she'll have to go to wide-screen TV."

Of course Ms. Mansfield went on to say better and nicer things about Oprah, but then reverted back to her problem with weight again, "She is gorgeous and knows it. She is wearing a royal blue jersey and tight matching pants. Her hips are the size of a Castro convertible."

Though Oprah takes the good comments along with the bad, which is an ever-present faction of her personality, sometimes the comments she receives are pretty darn harsh. However, leaving Oprah's size out of a description of her would be like leaving out the fact that she's a woman. The description would be incomplete.

Oprah brings up the topic of her weight on her show, now and then. Instead of ignoring or trying to hide her problem with overeating, she chooses to cleanse herself of her guilt by sharing her diets with her audience. Often, she'll do shows on overeating, dieting, or weight-related cosmetic surgery. She has even gone as far as to offer to diet along with her guests, and they join her. Once an audience that was mostly all overweight wore shirts emblazened with the slogan DIET WITH OPRAH.

Being overweight isn't exclusive to Oprah. When she hears a guest sadly relate that she lost tens of pounds, only to gain it all back in a few short weeks, Oprah understands. She's been there. More than once.

Oprah seems to love eating food as much as she enjoys abstaining from it. She has tried almost every diet known to the overweight: the Stillman Diet, Atkins, Beverly Hills,

Fit for Life, etc. She even claims to have gained several pounds while on the Scarsdale Diet.

On a recent *Oprah Winfrey Show*, while interviewing a plastic surgeon, Oprah wanted to ask a question about the liposuction technique but feared people would think she wanted the information for her personal benefit. She said, "The last time we did one of these shows, a couple weeks after I had asked a question about liposuction, one of the tabloids said, 'Oprah Winfrey considers risky liposuction surgery, fiancé Stedman Graham demands she suck sixty pounds from her body.' I'm not considering it, I'm just asking the question."

In more stressful, earlier times, Oprah binged on whatever foods were available. Once, when nothing else was available, she ate all that was handy: frozen hotdog buns dipped and swirled in a pool of Log Cabin maple syrup.

Though Oprah's past food binges can be considered pretty excessive, she tries to keep a closer eye on what she eats now while keeping an open mind about what she can and cannot do. She told Stephanie Mansfield, "I know I cannot deprive myself and be the same person. I have to figure out a way to do it." Perhaps, with the loving and loyal support of a good man in her life, Oprah just may take a realistic approach to her dieting. With that kind of incentive, sometime in the future we may see a streamlined Oprah Winfrey, once again.

Though she has plenty of her own problems, Oprah never ceases to come to the aid of others. Sometimes all that people need to solve their problems is someone to show them the way. With Oprah's example to follow, many a young girl has been led from poor and pitiful circumstances into real lives, rich with the encouragement and faith of someone who cares about their future.

Oprah will often speak free of charge to groups of young people with a new, understanding way of doing things. Her contributions so far have been immeasurable. She works with a group of teens who are caught in the same type of social traps that she experienced while living

with her mother. The girls are poor, lonely; some have
been abused, as she was. Taking the lead, as her father,
Vernon Winfrey, did with her, Oprah encourages achievement. In fact she uses many of the same methods by
having the girls do book reports, learn new words and ways
to use them. Oprah doesn't use the threat of 'going to bed
without supper' as her father did; however, she does use
money as an incentive. Having learned the valuable lessons her father set forth in her youth, Oprah Winfrey takes
the girls' problems deep into her heart. Though she understands the young teens' needs (whether the girls know
what those needs are or not), she's now able to stand at
some distance as she takes in the big picture.

She spends three to four days a week speaking at churches,
youth organizations, and shelters for the impoverished.
Oprah extends her warmth even further than that, spending
yet another two days a week with her "Little Sisters"
group at the Cabrini-Green housing projects in Chicago.
Her devotion to these young girls is relentless. The most
talked-about topic between Oprah and her 'little sisters' is
pregnancy. The best way to deal with teenage pregnancy
in poverty-stricken areas is through education and understanding. Without the knowledge of basic human biology,
it is most difficult for young people to deal with their
sexuality effectively.

Oprah Winfrey understands full well the harsh realities
of biological ignorance and the lack of honest information.
Shortly after several sexual attacks, when she was a child,
Oprah learned 'the facts of life' in school. With the sudden
knowledge of 'where babies come from', she feared an
imminent birth. Certain that she would give birth at any
time (she wasn't, in fact, pregnant at all), Oprah would
often leave class and rush into the girl's lavatory so she
could "have it in there." She would rather have had a
baby in the cold school bathroom than to have anyone find
out about her sexual molestations.

Oprah's TV staff sometimes joins her on her frequent
trips to the Cabrini-Green projects. These projects are

smack in the middle of Chicago's worst area. Long known for crime, drugs, deaths, beatings and shootings, the place is a montage of society's cruelest and lowliest debaucheries. Almost daily media reports attest to that. The "Little Sisters" group Oprah formed is made up of about twenty-five young girls who live there.

As part of her efforts to help young people, Oprah took her program cast and crew to the Cabrini-Green projects to show the horrible living conditions, though not all of them agreed to go with her. The result was somber and telling. Here again Oprah seems to be one of the few TV personalities to bring the rarely seen lives of those who suffer, while others feast, to the public's awareness.

On the poverty-stricken ghettos of Chicago's West Side, Oprah told her audience: "In this part of town in Chicago, where if you had any choice at all, you would not want to be. And if you had any choice at all, you would not want to live. It is one of the most impoverished urban areas in the country, and it's right in my own backyard. It's probably no different than the ghetto in the city where you live. The most remarkable fact about American poverty now is that we're all getting used to it. It has become a permanent fixture in our everyday lives, although sometimes we go quite out of our way not to drive through those unsavory blocks where the poor reside. By steering clear of those areas it's often a way of trying to forget that they exist. But poor America has been with us since the birth of this country, and it's not going away."

"Most people want to forget these people, the permanent underclass exist. We are attempting to take all the meaningless headlines that we read daily, and bring them to life, by introducing you, face to face, to poverty."

She's had some of "her" teens from the Cabrini-Green projects over to her home for pajama parties and other intimate get-togethers. In 1976 Oprah took two of the girls with her on a trip to Nashville. Each girl got $25 from Oprah, with the provision that during the excursion, whenever one of them made a grammatical error, they had to return one of the dollars. Another provision supplied by the ever aware Winfrey was that whenever she used bad grammar herself, such as saying 'Yeah' instead of the correct affirmation 'Yes,' she would give each of them one dollar.

Oprah shows the girls a good time by taking them to parties and plays, but her time with them isn't always an enjoyable experience. She always manages to come up with Oprahistic lessons, that turn and lead the girls toward a more prosperous and educated future.

She told Joan Barthel, "I shoot a very straight shot: 'Get pregnant and I'll break your face!' Don't tell me you want to do great things in your life and still not be able to tell a boy no. You want something to love and hug, tell me, and I'll buy you a puppy."

"When we talk about goals, and they say they want Cadillacs, I say, 'If you cannot read or do math, if you become pregnant, if you drop out of school, you will never own a Cadillac, I guarantee it! And if you get any D's or F's on your report card, you're out of this group. Don't tell me you want to do great things in your life if all you carry to school is a radio.' "

Oprah is not blind to the obstacles these young girls have in front of them. "We have twenty-four in our group. Maybe we'll save two." One girl confided to Oprah that she wanted to have lots of babies so that she would collect more money from the state welfare system. As difficult as this kind of behavior is to overcome, she remains undaunted. Imagine if those close to her had given up on Oprah. Because of Oprah Winfrey, we just may be welcoming a new set of young people who have broken their circumstantial bonds to become successful, intelligent citizens. Her belief is to overcome and achieve, and no contribution is too small. On the other hand, no contribution is too large. In 1986 Oprah joined many others and went to Ethiopia to do whatever she could to help the starving people there.

All this, and she still has time for her career, friends,

and most recently, Stedman Graham. Without a doubt, Oprah Winfrey is one of the busiest TV star/humanitarians we have in this country, even though her humanitarian efforts are seldom recognized. Such a full and devoted existence leaves little time for self-doubt. She tries not to let the little things bother her, as she did in the past. Today her life is a far cry from the days when she sobbed on her knees and considered suicide.

Oprah spoke of her busy schedule in *Woman's Day*: "My friends are office people. We work and we go out to dinner and talk about work. Then we go home and we're back here about 7:30 in the morning. This is all I do," she continues. "I do this and I do it till I drop. I work, and on weekends I go as many places as I can to speak. I get home and I say, 'What am I supposed to do here?' I guess I could go to the movies. I could. I could do that." Does she go to the movies? "I don't."

Having filled a longstanding void in Oprah Winfrey's heart, Stedman Graham has made her life much more pleasurable. Her previous relationships (or lack of them) caused such an emotional turmoil that, for a while, she hung on the brink of suicide. When Oprah attempted suicide she was at the sore end of a long-term relationship. Having treated her with little respect or caring, her boyfriend left her; she felt scared and alone. "I had so much going for me," Oprah said. She was already earning a whopping six-figure income, and was about to make her big move to Chicago.

"I still thought I was nothing without a man. I'd had a relationship with a man for four years (I wasn't living with him, I've never lived with anyone) and I thought I was worthless without him. The more he rejected me, the more I wanted him. I felt depleted, powerless. Once I stayed in bed for three days, missing work; I just couldn't get up."

"I don't think I was really serious about suicide, but I wrote my best friend a note. It was Saturday, around 8:30. I'd been down on the floor, crying. I told her where my insurance policies were, and I asked her to take care of my

plants. I came across the note just lately—this is the first
time I've talked about it—and I cried for the woman I was
then." How many 'Oprahs' have we lost, in the struggle it
takes to overcome our saddest and loneliest times? Probably far too many than we have deserved.

Although Oprah managed not to succumb to her suicidal
wish, she carries that memory with her, too, as a constant
reminder of where she was as a woman then and where she
is as a woman today. "I was so adamant about being my
own person that I wouldn't go for counseling. Then it
came to me: I realized there was no difference between me
and an abused woman who has to go to a shelter, except I
could stay home. It was emotional abuse, which happens
to women who stay in relationships that do not allow for
them to be all that they can be. You're not getting knocked
around physically, but in terms of your ability to soar,
your wings are clipped."

Free to live her life to its full potential, with regard for
her sisters who all deserve to reach their full human potential but are held back by closely conditioned relationships,
Oprah talks about her past reluctance to achieve. "Women
have that common bond when it comes to giving up power.
I speak to a lot of women now, trying to get them to
understand that each of us is responsible for herself. You
can read that in books, but it isn't until you come to a
spiritual understanding of who you are—not necessarily a
religious feeling, but deep down, the spirit within—that
you can begin to take control."

With only herself at the controls, and maybe a helpful
hint from Stedman Graham, Oprah is well on her way to
becoming a pure individual. "I had given this man (prior
boyfriend) the power over my life." Vowing to keep her
personal responsibilities her own, she said, "I will never,
never—as long as I am black!—I will never give up my
power to another person." Feeling a little better she adds,
"Now I'm free. I'm soaring."

Today Oprah has the courage to stand on her own as a
successful and confident human being, barely pausing to

dwell on the intense learning phases of her life. The more that happens to her, the more she is able to surpass and learn. As a talk show host, Oprah's past plays a predominant role in her compatibility with an ever-growing audience. To learn from one's mistakes is why you must endure them. To learn enough from them to grow and adapt is far better than just remembering them. Oprah uses her past experiences to broaden, even further, her seemingly blessed adulthood.

Without a firm understanding of your own humanity, it is difficult to understand the inner workings of others. With that understanding sometimes comes humor. When Oprah Winfrey decided to go to Ethiopia to do her best for the starving millions there, she had to take another look at herself. What would the poor, starvation-bloated people of Ethiopia think about an overweight American who walked through their towns rich with the food of prosperity? Oprah suffered many a jab from colleagues and friends about her trip to Ethiopia. Two weeks before she was to appeaar on the *Tonight Show* for the first time, Oprah left for sunny Ethiopia.

Some of her staff thought that such a depressing trip would lead Oprah into depression because of the supreme difficulty of trying to help the countless lives that suffered in Ethiopia. Oprah reassured them that whatever the outcome, she'd still be the same Oprah Winfrey she was before she left. Still, some had their doubts, and rightly so. The devastation and starvation in Ethiopia staggers the mind, hundreds of thousands of human lives wasting in the African deserts. Oprah would talk about the feelings those people had, about her changing after serving an extended amount of time within such waste and destruction.

Debbie DiMaio, as quoted by Robert Waldron, said, "Given those conditions in Ethiopia, I was concerned that if she can feel for one person, I cannot imagine Oprah with thousands and thousands of starving people that were about to die. I think she's like a sponge, and to have all those emotions pounded into her . . . I was just a little concerned."

Oprah's response to her friend was, "You don't know me well if you think Oprah will come back and she won't be bubbly anymore." She knew that such an experience would lead to a more enlightened understanding of the sufferings that were, and are, so much a part of life in Ethiopia.

Her first day in the city was all too revealing to Oprah, who immediately felt the burden each citizen needed to endure in order to sustain their existence. With the sight of small children carrying heavy loads of wood on their frail backs, in the hope of raising the few cents that might buy a small portion of food, Oprah's empathetic abilities began to surface. She couldn't help but notice that small children, teens, and adults were literally dying on their feet while continuing the time-tested struggle of acquiring a day's pitiful food allotment. Along with heavy pounds of wood, these children carried the burden of fighting to stay alive.

As uninspiring as her initial confrontation with the hump-backed poor was, Oprah continued her tour, undaunted. She was led to a section of the city that sat above the impoverished dwellings below. From there, the entire city and surrounding area was visible. The camera crew chose this place for a series of shots showing the expanse and sparsity of Ethiopia's vastness. While there, Oprah was confronted by a small swarm of Ethiopian children. They quickly trotted over, with the packs of wood still strapped to their young backs, and immediately began begging. They approached the crew, each applying his own special begging methods. They tried Oprah (they must have known she was a soft touch!) but unfortunately she didn't have any money with her. All of the cash had been left back at the hotel. Who needs money when you're climbing a hill? The biggest pleasure Oprah and her empty-pocketed crew could offer them was a few small bottles of Coca-Cola.

This was to the poor children not only a supreme gesture of friendship but a wide-eyed introduction to some of the most distant, and unreachable, taste sensations. Imagine a starving child happily sipping at a glassy bottle of Coke. The gifts went over well with the children. They grinned and pranced at the soft drinks, and Oprah was glad to have brought at least something to their daily trauma. "What I understood on that hill is that, one at a time, we can make a difference. It sounds trite. But for some reason that thought occurred to me, that you really can. You really, really can. You can't take every child out of the hills of Ethiopia, but you can do what you can to make a difference."

Oprah also received some pressure from people about why she chose to leave the country to help Ethiopia's needy when so many of our own population are in the same dire straights. Oprah let them know where she stood on that matter. "I really think the problem of starvation and famine far exceeds anything."

Oprah speaks realistically of the experience of death in Ethiopia. "The basic human rights to food and shelter are denied. I mean, children freeze. Most of the people die between four and five in the morning because that's when it's coldest in the desert. You die because there's not a blanket. So you understand a lot about the world . . . what matters and what doesn't."

Oprah likened the efforts of WLS-TV and the Chicago viewers who supported her trip to Ethiopia to a kind of Band-Aid, because "without the rest of the world, without us, a people would've died. It's so clear. You understand that nobody else is doing anything, that the Ethiopian government is not, for whatever reasons, political or otherwise, so we really have made a difference." In a sometimes cruel and unforgiving world, it's nice to know that there are people like Oprah Winfrey. And it's a good thing that some of those people are rich.

Oprah was never one to scorn charity; in fact she gives the most a human has to give: her time, her understanding, and lots of money. This may seem like an invitation to those who might try to fake a need, confronting her in order to assimilate some of her hard-earned funds. Oprah has a practical rule that she'll donate money only if she hasn't been asked for it. This rule keeps her one up on the greedy self-interest groups that sometimes approach her. Still, Oprah keeps an open mind and an open eye. When she sees that she can truly be of help to one human being, or a thousand, she is ready to give the hardest thing there is to give: yourself.

After her strenuous journey to hot, barren Ethiopia, Oprah settled back into her normal lifestyle. *The Oprah Winfrey Show* was as popular as ever, and she had a new message to bring to her followers. Oprah never misses a chance to bring new understanding to those who are so disconnected (yet as human beings, so intimately connected) with the honorless horrors of the northern African famine. "Although the people are being fed over there, they're fed and then they wait for their next feeding. What I understand is, unless you create a society in which people can take care of themselves, and be responsible for themselves, then you really basically have no society." Surely a point of Oprah's fine-tuning. She continues, "So what's the point? The point is to keep people from starving, obviously. But the point also is to set up some kind of educational system so that people can better themselves. And you can only do that through knowledge. You just can't do that sitting on a hill weaving baskets."

2

Big Time

"Everything that you are right now is a composite of everything that has happened to you in the past."

—OPRAH WINFREY

In early 1985, Quincy Jones, best known for his musical compositions and as a big-time record producer, saw *The Oprah Winfrey Show* on a hotel television while visiting Chicago. Jones needed only a few minutes of watching the program to realize that the woman he saw before him was the perfect woman to play the character Sophia in his new film project, *The Color Purple*. Quincy Jones and co-producer Stephen Spielberg (whose most notable past productions include *E.T.*, *Jaws*, *Raiders of the Lost Ark*, *Indiana Jones and the Temple of Doom*) made arrangements for Oprah to audition for the film. Due to her incredible acting talents and personal charms, she was awarded the part of Sophia, the daughter-in-law of the central character.

Though Oprah was thrilled with such a high-ranking role in *The Color Purple*, she would have been just as happy with being an errand-girl, or water-woman. She had read Alice Walker's novel *The Color Purple* with great interest. Not only had she long admired Alice Walker's soul-reaching works, she had a particular attachment to this special story of the pre-war South. She would have done anything to become part of such an exciting, emotionally wrought motion picture.

Hailed as an achievement not only for blacks but for the entire film industry as well, *The Color Purple* received eleven Academy Aware nominations as well as Golden Globe nominations. Winfrey herself was nominated for Best Supporting Actress by the Academy, and she received numerous other nominations and awards for her part in the film. In January 1987, Oprah received two prestigious Image Awards given by the N.A.A.C.P. to recognize and honor black entertainers who project a positive black image. Most recipients receive the Image Award after their efforts have been overlooked by other award ceremonies. Not only did Oprah Winfrey win an Image Award for her role as Sophia in *The Color Purple*, she also received one for her syndicated talk show, *The Oprah Winfrey Show*, which was named by the N.A.A.C.P. as "The Best News or Information Series."

Oprah's former drama instructor from Tennessee State University, Dr. William Cox, told me his feelings about Oprah's double N.A.A.C.P. awards. "I know she deserved both," he said. In Dr. Cox's opinion, the better of the two, with respect to being an inspiration to blacks, was for the movie. "If I must choose one above the other, it would be *The Color Purple*. This movie was so popular in Nashville it was held over for seven weeks. It was an inspiration to our students in the theater."

During her years at Tennessee State University, Oprah spent many long hours with her mentor, Dr. Cox, developing her natural and wonderfully gifted talents. He encouraged Oprah's father to allow Oprah to attend overnight theatrical trips and was successful in most every attempt. The stern Vernon Winfrey needed constant prodding to let his daughter out of his home after the now well-established curfew, yet according to Dr. Cox, "Her father and mother attended every performance that I had responsibility for." Vernon Winfrey accepted Oprah's choice to pursue an acting career, although reluctantly; his love for her preceded any feeling or need he had to control her.

Though Dr. Cox is a veteran theatrical director and drama coach, he is not immune to Oprah's ability to bring him, as a viewer, close to tears. He told me, "Since I have been in theater for over thirty years, it is difficult for me to empathize in something I am a part of, but Oprah almost got to me in the scene where she was knocked to the ground by the white man in *The Color Purple*. What saved me," he said fondly, "was when Oprah realized her underclothing was being photographed and she made a slight movement to cover it. I have teased her about that scene."

Oprah hasn't called Dr. Cox for some time, though there was a time when the two would often confer. When she was calling him on a semi-regular basis, they talked about personal matters, rarely exchanging professional advice. Dr. Cox says, "We did talk briefly while I was in Chicago at a drama conference about her trip to New York concerning her television program while making *The Color Purple*. I told her if necessary to grab the movie even if she had to neglect the show." Neither *The Color Purple* nor *The Oprah Winfrey Show* suffered from Oprah's choice to spread herself thin by continuing to do both.

Dr. Cox is not against Oprah's success as a television talk-show personality, but he maintains his highest respect for her acting talents, which he was so much a part of helping to develop. When I asked him if he sees any of himself or his teachings in Oprah's present-day dramatic performances, he responded, "I think Oprah had all the tools I am accused of having. I probably helped her to hone them. She was endowed with a sense of humor that was backed up by curtness. We both practice punctuality, and are both too stubborn to quit until the job is done. This I learned from my days in the Marine Corp."

"I have learned many things from having taught Oprah," Dr. Cox said. "I am still learning from Oprah and I use her past and present life to motivate and stimulate my students. Since we are a predominantly Black university, nothing can be more inspiring to a Black student than to have an internationally known Black person to use as a model."

On the success rate of the drama department at Tennessee State University, Dr. Cox says, "We have a few successful thespians from our department, namely, Moses Gunn (*Father Murphy*), Leon Summers (*Dream Girls*), Alonso Ward (*Jaws III*)." Alonso Ward and Oprah Winfrey attended Tennessee State University at the same time, starring together in numerous T.S.U. productions. One was a play called *The Martin Luther King Story* in which Oprah was Coretta King and Alonso Ward was Dr. Martin Luther King, Jr. The play was written by Ellwoodson Williams, a former student at Tennessee State. Both Alonso and Oprah conferred with the author during their adaptation of his work.

Dr. Cox once told Robert Waldron that Alonso Ward and Oprah were very close friends, but he was not "her boyfriend." "He was a companion. One night she came in wearing high-heel shoes," referring to the pre-production of *The Martin Luther King Story*. "Alonso wasn't as tall as Oprah and was very much alarmed about the situation. He felt Coretta King shouldn't overshadow her husband by being taller than he was. Eventually they worked it out."

While many of our former students are lawyers, judges, and Ph.D's teaching in many of the major universities, Dr. Cox always keeps a warm place in his heart for Oprah Winfrey. He said, "Many of her friends have a warm feeling about her many endeavors. She has excelled in motion pictures and T.V. We are hoping she will become a "ham" (that she is!) for the stage. Her humanitarian activities are too numerous to mention. I get long distance calls from my former students telling me how great she was as a speaker for many charitable occasions. Some of these calls, however, were collect calls," he says curtly.

Dr. Cox considers Oprah's greatest humanitarian gesture to be a large donation she made to the students and future students of Tennessee State University. "She gave our school $50,000 to be used for ten $5,000 scholarships in her father's name (Vernon Winfrey). She has made a commitment to donate $200,000 at a later date. All I've got to say," Dr. Cox says with his wit in check, "is if she has that kind of money, please send me that dime for that telephone call and the dollar I sent (her) when her phone was disconnected."

In the film adaptation of *The Color Purple,* Oprah Winfrey played Sophia, a large, busty Southern woman. Sophia made it clear at a young (and pregnant) age that she would have no part in sexist, racist, or physically abusive behavior toward herself. When confronted with such behavior, she fought back, with a hefty and powerful punch. Eventually, her aggressive, anti-abusive reaction got her into far more trouble than she had anticipated. She was the wife of Celie's stepson. Celie, the central focus of the film, was played wonderfully by Whoopi Goldberg. Celie was forced to do the bidding of her cruel and vicious husband after her sex-hungry father gave her to him. She was to endure frequent beatings and psychological traumas during her forced relationship, which bordered on violently aggressive slavery. Sexually used and lowlier than a dog, Celie eventually overcame her master and left to live with her sister Nettie on her dead father's farm.

Oprah's supporting role as Sophia showed her capabilities as a true, common-bond professional actress. She lived the entire life of Sophia in front of your eyes, and the audience often left the picture wondering how their good friend Sophia would do. After walloping a white man in the face with her fist, Sophia is accosted by an angry group of upper-class whites. A policeman runs up to the crowd, now surrounding the frightened Sophia like a circle of death. The policeman quickly lifts his hand and ham-

mers her in the face with his service revolver. Sophia is
then jailed for many years, even though she had been hit
first; she finally leaves the confines of prison broken and
lifeless.

Oprah's Sophia is the portrait of a woman brave enough
to stand up to any human being, only to be systematically
reduced to a cowering, frightened blob of servitude. She
didn't even recognize her own children. Only the eventual
rise and change of Celie's slavish relationship with her
husband brings Sophia out of her loss of freedom's faith,
and she returns to her former robust, bustling lifestyle.
Oprah is excellent in *The Color Purple*. She brings us the
inner workings of a woman-triumphant.

At one time, part of the N.A.A.C.P. felt that the film
didn't do justice to blacks. Since the violent and sexually
abusive behavior of some of the characters was shown
without softening any blows, they worried that *The Color
Purple* would show blacks in a bad light. Later on, though,
the N.A.A.C.P. majority decision was that *The Color
Purple* was, in fact, good—so good that a total of three
Image Awards was given to the film, surpassed only by
the ever popular television program, *The Cosby Show*,
which received four awards that year.

The Color Purple was Oprah Winfrey's first major motion picture screen role, but she was a well-developed
actress before. During her early days at Tennessee State
University, Oprah performed numerous stage roles which,
in some people's minds, were equal to her portrait of
Sophia in *The Color Purple*. Drawing on her past experience, and on her feelings of being a modern black woman,
enabled Oprah to play the omniscient role of a struggling
black woman in a racist, impoverished existence. Sophia
was a sometimes mean yet strikingly clear woman who
never let her strong feelings as a free soul escape her, as
she battled jail and oppression in her fictional life. "I
don't think of myself as a poor deprived ghetto girl who
made good," she told Joan Barthel. "I think of myself as

somebody who from an early age knew I was responsible for myself, I *had* to make good."

Winfrey had plenty of personal experience to draw from, having endured beatings at the hands of her grandmother, sexual abuse, and poverty as a child. "I understand my commonality with the human experience," Oprah said to Thomas Morgan. "We all want to be happy, we have sad times. If you have lived, you have overeaten at one period or another. I'm not afraid to show those feelings. I can say, 'Look, I have been there. I understand how it feels to be in love with somebody and not have him love you back.' People say, 'Doggone that Oprah, isn't she something?' But they don't realize sometimes that I'm just like them." Describing one of the scenes from *The Color Purple,* Oprah continues, "Mine was the last angle to be shot. I had been sitting there watching everybody else. I had a lot of time to think about the years Sophia spent in jail, and how thousands of women marched in Selma who were thrown in jail and what those years must have been like."

"Sophia finally speaking was a victory for all of us, and for me," Oprah said. "I had in the back of my mind Fannie Lou Hamer." Fannie Lou Hamer was a civil rights leader in rural Mississippi, during the sixties, who had also led a troubled life. Oprah told Joan Barthel, "I had Fannie Lou Hamer in the back of my head. I thought of her being in and out of jail, so brutalized. I'm aware of my legacy, which is why I was honored to play Sophia. She was a part of all those women I'd been carrying around with me for years. In high school oratory contests, while everybody did a speech from *Inherit the Wind,* I'd be doing something from Alice Walder's *Jubilee,* about a slave woman after the Civil War, or Sojourner Truth's *Ain't I a Woman* speech."

Fearing someone might get the wrong impression, and think Oprah Winfrey a hard-core black activist, she says she doesn't act in order to "remind people that I'm black. Race is not an issue with me. In school, when the other black kids were organizing a bloc vote for student council, I didn't vote with them because I thought their candidate wasn't the best qualified. I was ostracized then; they called me 'Oreo'." "But I've always believed, as Jesse Jackson says, that "excellence is the best deterrent to racism and sexism; that the greatest contribution you can make to woman's rights, to civil rights, is to be the absolute damndest best at what you do."

She once said, "This whole path to success is not as difficult as some people would want you to believe. The process was the goal, and I've taken great joy in the process. My main concern about myself now is whether I will live up to my potential; I already reach more people than politicians do." Audrey Edwards, editor of *Essence*, called Oprah Winfrey "the only black woman currently enjoying fame in both television and film." Oprah told her, "I always knew that whatever I wanted for myself I could get."

"There were certainly times as a child when I felt, 'My God, I wish I were like everybody else,' but as an adult, I celebrate my upbringing. I say, 'Thank goodness I was raised by my grandmother, then sent to live with my mother then with my father.' Because of the various environments I was exposed to, I am better able to understand what others have gone through." Oprah confided to Chris Andersen, "Everything that happens to you happens for a reason—everything you do in your life comes back to you. I call it 'Divine Reciprocity'. That's why I try to be kind to people—more for myself than for them."

Her methods seem to be working for her. Oprah has been getting just what she's been wanting. She had read *The Color Purple* and knew, somehow, she'd like to be a part of it. The surprise came when she heard that the book was to be made into a motion picture. Just as she was about to contact the studio, co-producer Quincy Jones called. "I had read Alice Walker's novel and was just floored with it. When I heard that they were going to make a movie of it, I thought, 'Oh, Lord, I will do anything to

be involved—anything!' Then Quincy Jones called. It was
my true destiny.'' To this day Oprah refers to Jones as her
''Number one favorite person in the universe'' (aside from
Mr. Graham, no doubt).

Oprah didn't just breeze through the filming of *The
Color Purple* though. At times there were tense moments
and tight situations. ''For the first time in my life I thought,
What if I do my best and it's just not good enough?'' she
fretted. As you already know, her performance was better
than ''just good enough.'' It was outstanding. Oprah's
Sophia received applause from critics and audiences alike.
The Color Purple is now available on video-cassette, so
this film will continue to reach an even broader audience.
When asked which she prefers, movies or television, Winfrey
said, ''Both, with a difference. I'm a good interviewer
largely because I taught myself how, but I was born to
act.''

''I believe I am the seed of the free,'' Oprah brazenly
told Thomas Morgan. ''I believe these women (Celie,
Sophia, Nettie) are a part of my legacy and the bridges that
I crossed to get where I am today. They are looking out for
me.''

Her next film project was *Native Son*, written by novel-
ist Richard Wright in 1940. This fine film received much
less acclaim and attention than its predecessor had. Though
in the minds of many, her role in *Native Son* was far
superior to the role of Sophia, the film didn't please
audiences like *The Color Purple* did. Some even thought
her role too sentimental. *Native Son* is about a young black
man (Bigger Thomas) who, through nervous ignorance,
accidentally kills the daughter of his employer. Oprah
played the murderer's mother, a give-anything, try-anything
parent, who begs on her knees that God will burden her
with her son's ensuing trial and incarceration. Bigger Thomas
was portrayed sympathetically as a victim of the racist,
Capitalist system. Wright, himself a practicing Communist
until his death in 1960, focused on Bigger as a socially
overconditioned man.

Peter Bergman called *Native Son* "Wright's greatest work." Other books written by Richard Wright have reached a high level of respect through the years. *Black Boy, Uncle Tom's Children*, and others have been mainstays of American black literature for decades. Bergman places Wright at the top of "the school of Chicago naturalists which began at the turn of the century with (authors) Theodore Dreiser and Frank Norris."

In what may be considered her finest acting performance, Oprah plays Mattie Michael, again the mother of a grown, wayward boy who finds himself in jeopardy with the law, in Gloria Naylor's *The Women of Brewster Place*, a story of seven women who share their lives and living quarters. The tale is considered a new American classic, showing the traumatic, poignant living conditions and feelings of different women caught in a poverty-stricken life. Oprah is on both sides of the production, both acting and starring in *The Women of Brewster Place*. Certainly this is a chance for Oprah Winfrey to prove herself as more than a pretty face. What great and wonderful parts she has yet to play is in the bountiful hands of the future.

6

The Oprah Winfrey Show

*"It's . . . a kick to walk into a Dairy Queen in, say,
Lexington, Kentucky, and have somebody say, 'Hey
Ofrey, I saw you on T.V. this morning!' "*

—OPRAH WINFREY

On September 8, 1986 Oprah's syndicated King World
placed *The Oprah Winfrey Show* in an unprecedented 138
cities across the United States. With a profit earnings
estimate of 125 million dollars for the 1987-88 season and
150 million dollars for the 1988-89 season, it is under-
standable that such a mighty syndicate as King World
would pick up and distribute the show, adding it to its long
string of successful television shows. Of that incredible
profit estimate, Oprah stands to rake in massive dollars
herself. King World wasn't actually going out on a limb by
accepting *The Oprah Winfrey Show*. Oprah already had a
well-proven television track record, having beaten all other
programs in her time slot by lengths.

"Ain't it somethin'? I feel as good as you can feel and
still live," she once told Audrey Edwards in *Essence*.

"Really. I mean there are some days when I'm thinking, 'If it gets any better, I may just jump over the moon.' "

Edwards says, "Oprah knows that her best strategy for succeeding is to just go on doing what she has always done so well—be herself, a big and pretty black woman who is smart, talented, and naturally endowed with the gift of gab and the capacity to make others feel at ease."

"If Oprah could be stereotyped," said Edwards, "it might be easy to explain her crossover success as representing America's love for the quintessential mammy figure—the big warm Black woman who is a natural in a medium as intimate as the television talk-show format. But Oprah is too good, too much a genuine original, to be stereotyped. Like any other celebrity, Oprah has had her share of criticism—largely from other Blacks. There are those who say she panders to white folks, that she is too much the rah-rah girl and not enough of the down-home sister. People tend to be suspicious when Blacks appear to be too beloved by whites."

"I have the ability to be myself in front of the camera, which is a gift," she revealed to Thomas Morgan. "So many other people play television: they sit a certain way, talk a certain way, even if the set is falling down. Vulnerability is the key; people appreciate when you can be honest. It lets them feel more comfortable about being themselves."

Oprah and her fine staff have made extensive progress in the never-ending search for guests and talent that are unique, and for topics that even the wierdest of us could relate to in some way or another. The variety is staggering. She's had famous actors on her show, like Tom Selleck; politicians such as Jesse Jackson; numerous doctors and other professionals; members and former members of organizations such as the Ku Klux Klan; fashion models, nudists, and hired killers. In a recent conversation, the infamous Jimmy 'the Weasle' Fratianno mentioned to Oprah that one of his intended victims of a potential Mafia 'hit' was Desi Arnez. Only a fluke of circumstance save Arnez from the contractual killing. The person who wanted Desi killed went to jail; when he got out, he forgot that he had hired the Weasel to do in Arnez. Then he left the country and Jimmy 'the Weasel' never bothered to make the hit.

A *Newsweek* feature article about Oprah Winfrey said, "The on-camera Winfrey may be the most spontaneous force in all of videoland. Mischievously pressing Dudley Moore about the technical problems he encounters when sleeping with taller women, choking up over the plight of a homeless drifter, coquettishly coming on to Tom Selleck, pointedly inquiring of Ku Klux Klan members. Her followers delight in exchanging Oprah-isms, like the time that a visiting sociologist described how a roommate situation could evolve into a lesbian relationship and Oprah emphatically responded, 'Then I'm never getting a roommate.' Or the time she bluntly asked a porn-movie star: 'Don't you get sore?' "

Thomas Morgan wrote, "On the strength of her ratings against Mr. Donahue in Baltimore, Dennis Swanson, then general manager of WLS-TV in Chicago, named her host of *A.M. Chicago* in January 84. Station officials said that in the first ratings period after her arrival, Miss Winfrey's show captured the top spot in its time period and has beaten the Donahue show ever since."

Cathleen Schine wrote this in the May 1986 issue of *Vogue*: "Oprah Winfrey is tremendously appealing on her Donahue clone, *The Oprah Winfrey Show*. Winfrey, who was up for an Academy Award for *The Color Purple*, has a kind of indomitable down-home manner on her show— get in here, come on, and sit right down; eat up, go ahead now, tell me, go on, tell Oprah what's on your mind. She enfolds the audience in a luxuriously prosaic compassion."

"Like Phil Donahue, Winfrey is a pilgrim with a microphone. She steps gently among the people, into the firey angers and misty longings of Chicago. And now, like Donahue, she's going national. I've always avoided these shows, as well as the more anonymous radio talk-shows they resemble. The sight of people bearing their lurid souls seemed pornographic—certainly not edifying, as admirers claimed.''

"I'm not sure which *The Oprah Winfrey Show* is—a little of both, I suppose—but watching it, I cried and laughed almost as much as Oprah herself. One guest was an exquisite-looking girl who sat beside her mother talking softly about her father and incest, a large tear rolling excruciatingly slowly, eloquently, down her cheek. 'I know it's hard to tell,' Winfrey murmured. Then she began to sob and took a break.''

"I can't imagine that this sort of intimate exposure could happen any place but in the United States. A battered woman who shot her husband—then a commercial. One day, an elderly black man who escaped a Southern lynching after the hood had been pulled over his head, the rope tightened around his neck. Another day, a lot of hilariously noisy women on diets. It is television *verité*, a bizarre ongoing documentary film of the saddest, dearest, inside pockets of the baggy American suit. Oprah Winfrey pokes and prods, and every lipstick-stained Kleenex comes fluttering out. If I were a member of the KGB, I would watch this show. I may watch it anyway.''

Oprah was talking with *Essence* about her ordeal with ten women of the Ku Klux Klan on her talk show. The white-robed women talked at length about their racist, white suprematist attitudes; Oprah went on asking biting and far-reaching questions about KKK practices and beliefs, just as she would question any of her other guests. She didn't cower, she didn't back off when it came to tense questions of the Klan's disturbed beliefs. Oprah treated them cordially, and with little malice. Whatever contempt she may have been feeling wasn't apparent on her face. On the other hand, she did get a little squirrelly toward the end of the interview, and playfully asked the Klan women if they would like to go out on the town with her after the show for a bite to eat. Oprah's lunch invitation didn't go over too well with the women, who declined her generous offer. They were even more ticked off when

Oprah announced to a gleeful audience that she would even pick up the tab; again they steadfastly refused.

She told Pamela Johns, "Some people said, 'I would have slapped them,' but what you must understand," she explained, "is that when the show is over, those people are still gonna be Klan girls and I'm still going to be Oprah. You can only hope to expose racism for what it is."

Joan Barthel said that "Oprah did not so much host the show as immerse herself in it, with a style that blended earthiness, humor, spontaneity, and candor with a unique personal touch."

"When agoraphobia was the topic, she involved the audience with a caller who was down on the floor with the telephone, not having left the house in weeks; she kept in contact with the woman, arranged help for her, and eventually brought her on the show—a communal victory. Some programs seemed outright stunts—guests who discussed nudism appeared in the nude—but viewers were delighted. At the end of the second ratings period, the program was in the lead, and never lost it."

Oprah knows that the reason her show is so popular is because of one big reason: Oprah Winfrey. "I don't wish to sound arrogant," she told Ms. Barthel, "But I don't think there's a problem with our show being successful . . . People are the same in Tucson and Spokane and Chicago, I think. Oh, it's going to be a kick to walk into a Dairy Queen in, say, Lexington, Kentucky, and have somebody say, 'Hey Ofrey, I saw you on T.V. this morning.' "

Not everyone was as pleased with Oprah's new talk show as *Newsweek* and *Vogue* had been. In a journalistic blast against *The Oprah Winfrey Show,* writer Lewis Grossberger of *Rolling Stone* treated his readers with this not-so-good review: "The Oprah Winfrey Show, the one new daytime talkie, is like watching Donahue with an imposter playing the role of Phil. The two shows are exactly the same: wandering host, smug experts, glum victims, jump-right-in audience, and all that endless jab-

bering about problems, problems, problems. Divorced trans-
vestites. Overweight claustrophobics. Schizophrenic step-
children of hearing-impaired Satan worshipers. . . ." Whew!
Something tells me that Grossberger didn't like what he
saw on *The Oprah Winfrey Show,* and he's not alone
apparently. Many viewers have expressed displeasure with
the format of the show and also have some unfounded
reasons to dislike Winfrey herself.

Oprah once spoke about some of the complaints she's
received for her interviewer's attitude. "You'll get a group
of sisters who say, 'Well, she don't look like nothing. I
don't see how she did it.' And now I get calls from people
who say to me, 'You know, you hug the white people
(during *The Oprah Winfrey Show*) more than you hug the
black people,' things like that. It's unfortunate, because
sometimes I feel that some black people really don't want
you to succeed. Some don't want you to go on the air and
just be yourself. They want a civil rights movement every
morning."

"I believe in excellence," Oprah told Mike Wallace of
60 Minutes, when he asked her why her television staff
was mostly white and female. "And the people I have are
excellent. I mean, it would be absolutely ridiculous to get
rid of these excellent people because they're white. That's
racism in reverse." Then, while trying to smooth things
with Wallace, she said, almost sheepishly, "When we
bring on additional staff, I will make sure that there's
some black people included." When Wallace mentioned
the possibility that her nationwide television program might
possibly fail, she said, "It'll do well, if it doesn't, I will
still do well. I will do well because I am not defined by the
show. I think we are defined by the way we treat ourselves
and the way we treat other people. It would be wonderful
to be acclaimed as this talk-show host who's made it. That
would be wonderful. But if it doesn't happen, there are
other important things in my life."

Oprah uses her program as a tool for the enlightenment
and benefit of her viewing audience. She brings forth the

things that are important to her, like the anti-drug benefits
she attends with her soulmate, Stedman Graham. "I don't
do drugs," she once said in *The Washington Post.* "I
don't need them. I'm not self-destructive." Then more
about the other aspects of herself: "I'm not a sleaze or a
slut. I say to them (her audience) I could not do what you
do. I can't bake a roast. I have not been to a grocery store
for two years. The last time I went grocery shopping, I
went on a vegetable kick and they all rotted. The broccoli
got so bad I had to call security to get it out."

However, Oprah Winfrey does have certain things in
common with her mostly female audience, "a belief system we all share in. I'm really no different from all of
those women who are watching because I want the same
things for my life that they want. I want to be happy, a
sense of fulfillment, children who love me, respect from
my husband."

Oprah's burst onto the TV scene began a continuing
stream of new talk-show clones. She has even been
accused of running competitor Phil Donahue right out of
Chicago. It is true that Mr. Donahue left the Windy City to
take his show *Donahue* to New York. Though both Oprah
Winfrey and Phil Donahue deny that this move was caused
by Oprah's incredible success, even with her staggeringly
high ratings in Chicago, there are still some who secretly
believe this was the case. Phil Donahue says that he
moved his program to New York for personal reasons
because his wife, Marlo Thomas, lived there. He has
mentioned this point over and over, but some people still
have their doubts.

"They said I was one of the reasons he moved to New
York," Oprah was quoted as saying in *Current Biography.*
"But I don't flatter myself; I know it was Marlo Thomas."
At a fancy farewell party in Chicago, during his last days
there, Phil Donahue told the crowd that he wished Oprah
well, "just not in (his) time slot."

"I would not be able to do my show if it were not for
Phil Donahue," Oprah told Joan Barthel. "Who thought

women were interested in talk-show subjects beyond how to put on mascara. I have the utmost respect for him.''

Oprah told Pamela Johns, when asked the amount of control she had over her show's content, "As much as I want. Nothing gets booked if I don't want to do it. It doesn't make sense to book it, because a lot depends on my interest and energy."

"I'm not a cupcake and I'm not a vanilla cream. I don't have thin lips and long blonde hair that I can wave out of my eyes, although I do bounce around as much as possible. It (*The Oprah Winfrey Show*) lets other women who look like me know that there are greater possibilities for them too. It all comes naturally. I'm blessed. Sometimes you don't choose your career; it chooses you."

Once people are satisfied that Oprah Winfrey is for real, as real as she seems, they can relax (or tighten up, depending on the guests) and get the substance of her hour-long program. She commands attention, with her black flame hair and inquisitive air. She knows what she'd like the guests to reveal, even if she couldn't have imagined the sometimes outrageous responses she receives.

People open up to Oprah Winfrey more than they do with any other talk-show host. It's her homey, prying charm that allows the guests to relieve themselves of harsh memories or revealing insights. "I feel like it's a ministry in many ways," Oprah told Stephanie Mansfield. "I certainly think of it as more than a talk show." Mansfield on Oprah Winfrey: "She's every woman's friend. The kind of brassy neighbor who barges into your house and immediately goes to the refrigerator for a little Cheez Whiz and bacon dip. And you love her for it. Because when you tell her you were molested by your doctor or you haven't spoken to your mother in a year, she understands."

Now, with considerable time on the air behind her, Oprah says, "I'm calmer. I think it's because I'm just trying to behave myself. I feel that I'm just visiting people's homes now for the first time. I don't immediately go to the refrigerator until I've gotten to know you. Then

I'll just go in and help myself.'' However, when the show was still a Chicago exclusive, she ''could say anything. Just about. People would know that just because I mentioned the word 'penis' I'm not a slut.''

Who could forget the hysterically classic lines she delivered during the show when the subject of discussion was 'penis size'—size, lengths of, enjoyment factors, preference, etc. Oprah revealed some of herself as she gushed out loud, ''If you had your choice, you'd like a big one if you could.'' The completely flabbergasted audience hooted and laughed as Oprah blurted out, ''Bring a *big* one home to mama!''

Something like that would ruin many a talk-show host's career, but the amusing Oprah Winfrey just adds the remark to her list of lines that keep her audience coming back. The audience loves it when she says something they've been thinking secretly for years. They love it when she steps out on a limb, half stumbling, yet in a quizzical kind of control. *Newsweek* said, ''Oprah's unique blend of folksy warmth and true grits frankness invariably wins forgiveness for such gaffes.''

Oprah comments on her vast audience: ''She's out there putting the laundry in. Sometimes I'll say 'Hold on, I'm trying to get your attention. I know you just took the roast beef out and you're trying to thaw it out.' I'm really fascinated by what people do in their lives all day. I could have a discussion all day with a housewife, saying, 'What do you do?' I'm not organized enough (to be a housewife). I never make the bed,'' she says. ''I figure I'll be back in it in 12 hours, so what's the point?''

''Would you like to tell us what is was like for you, Vicky, when you had your first orgasm?'' she asks of a young woman who was a guest on her show about sex-surrogates. Vicky paused briefly. Then she asked Oprah, ''Can I be explicit?'' ''Of course,'' Oprah nods. Vicky motioned toward her sex-surrogate. ''Well, he started by using his finger, very gently, inside me. I felt a slight contraction . . .'' Then came groans of unhappy stagehands and crew as they buried their faces in their hands. The stage manager ran down from his lofty control booth and made a frantic 'wrap' motion. Oprah, sensing that there may be major problems if she lets Vicky continue, says, "Thank you very much, Vicky, now we'll take a break."

While the hurriedly placed commercial plays, Oprah pivots around and once again confronts her audience. "When I said 'explicit', I didn't mean *that* explicit. Jesus Christ! Did I hold my face right?" The audience breaks into laughter; here again, Oprah isn't afraid to share her shock and dismay with her audience. She and the audience feel pretty much the same: nervous, giggly, and slightly uncomfortable. "Now the boss is downstairs screaming. So much for telling the truth. Lie a little!"

To the eye of a usually overprotected viewer, one who never gets to hear someone talk about orgasms or penis size, Oprah's show is a delight. To others, the last place they want to hear about women's sexual topics of discussion is on their kitchen-counter television. This and many other reasons make *The Oprah Winfrey Show* as popular as it is today. The freshness and upfront honesty with which pressing contemporary issues are dealt with are its main attraction, next to Oprah Winfrey.

After the show ended, Oprah had to face the program director, Tim Bennett. Bennett wasn't all too pleased with the things that were said on the show. Oprah said later that "management doesn't want problems, but they want ratings. I told them I'll be decent, and I was. They don't understand what women feel, and I do. Men think, for instance, that if you do a show about a mastectomy, you can't show a breast. I say you *have* to show a breast."

Oprah once told her audience, "There are millions of women who never experience sexual plesure. We had 633 calls from women yesterday, after the show, on the computer. We made lots of women feel they were not alone. It bothers me when we're accused of being sensational and exploitative. We are not. We are a caring group of people." She paused slightly. "Sometimes we make mistakes."

Stephanie Mansfield once said that "if Jane Pauley is the prom queen, Oprah Winfrey is the dorm counselor. People want to hold Barbara Walters' hand. They want to crawl into Oprah's lap."

"We go to the heart of the matter," Oprah Winfrey said in *Current Biography*. "We go for the absolute gut." When Oprah's guest was Jesse Jackson, she asked him if he had been nervous when talking to Mikhail Gorbachev, Mr. Jackson replied, "I was more nervous when I met you. You're more unpredictable," he said.

Oprah attributes the high level of success her show has received to herself and to following her own personal instincts. "Dishing out the dirt and meddling in other folk's business is what I do best. In acting you lose your personality in favor of the character you're playing, but you lose it to provide energy for your character. The same way on my show. I lose it and use it to concentrate on bringing the most out of my guests."

Often compared with Donahue, Oprah says, "Our format is the same, but the difference is in the field," she told Mark Christopher. "There's a different kind of emotion and involvement in my show. We're far more emotional. I don't know about Donahue," Oprah admitted. "I don't watch him. I don't know what his audience is doing. I hear myself being compared to him all the time. He was the one who first showed this country that women were bright and articulate and wished to be informed and were well-informed. He paved the way for moi. Before Donahue, you wouldn't have had that because programmers thought all women were interested in was how to do their mascara, where to put that blush, above the bone or below."

With more than a year of nationally syndicated television programs under her belt, Oprah continues her upward stride toward bigger and better success. The more she seems to do, the more money she makes. The more money she makes, the more she gives and helps. The more she gives to her charities and friends, the more fun she has. Her life appears to be an ever-growing circle of knowledge and good fortune. In our modern world, where the powerful-rich control many of our lives, it's to our benefit to encourage people like Oprah. It makes sense to let her do what she has to do. We can only gain from her experience and her ability to share her first-hand understanding.

She told Joan Barthel, "These have been the best years of my life. I swear, not a day goes by that I do not consciously say, 'Thank you. I'm truly blessed.' But I also believe that you tend to create your own blessings. You have to prepare yourself so that when opportunity comes, you're ready."

Knowing that there is more to her life than *The Oprah Winfrey Show*, Oprah realizes that her finest achievements to come are in her abilities as an actress. She also believes that occasionally there has been a certain degree of divine intervention. "*The Color Purple* was more than a lucky break," she once told Stephanie Mansfield. "I don't have to go and do *Raisin in the Sun* at community theaters because I know I can already do that. I know in my spirit I'm already an actress."

And she wants to be recognized as an actress. "So when you mention great actresses, you'll have to say my name; Meryl . . . Oprah . . . Hepburn . . . Oprah! That's what I want," she teases. "I was born to act."

Acting is in her blood, she has proven that, but when she takes a hand at the other side of performing, as the producer of *The Women of Brewster Place,* her horizons will open up even wider. It's hard to say what Oprah will be doing ten years from now. The possibilities are endless. Some things arre certain, though: Oprah will still be Oprah; she'll still have plenty to say and plenty to do. Her human-itarian efforts will have grown, and she will watch with pride and fondness the many results of her contributions to the human race.

The Woman of Brewster Place will be her first dramatic television acting performance. Oprah 'coming to TV' is like saying there are new clouds in the sky. She is already an integral part of it. The real treat will be Oprah giving her best big-screen portrait in the intimacy of in-home viewing. Even on television Oprah Winfrey is larger than life. She has already been seen in many television productions. Her face is recognizable to almost any television fanatic worth his/her mettle.

On the premiere of Dolly Parton's 1987 variety show, *Dolly,* Oprah made a guest appearance. She did a skit in which she played a black (imagine that) casting director for an upcoming production of *Porgy and Bess.* Dolly Parton played an aspiring actress who wanted to try out for the part of Bess. Oprah tried to hint to Dolly that she wasn't 'right' for the part. Dolly said, I've been singing *Summertime* all the way over here."

"I'm sorry, I am sorry," Oprah retorted, "but you are desperately wrong for this part." "How can you say that?" Dolly whimpered; "You didn't even hear me sing yet." "That will not be necessary." Dolly straightened up and shot back, "Oh sure, here it comes again. I heard it when I auditioned for *Dream Girls, Raisin in the Sun* and *The Wiz,* same old story . . . too short."

"Height has nothing to do with it," Oprah said in a matter-of-fact tone of voice. "Well, what is it then?" Dolly asked. "Well," Oprah paused. "You're very pretty, and you, uh . . . you have good energy and, uh, you're probably a fine actress and an accomplished singer; the problem is, wrong color."

Not wanting to lose her chance at the role, Dolly took Oprah's words to heart and quickly changed into a bright green dress. Early on in the show, Oprah and Dolly had a chance to talk before doing a rousing rendition of the gospel number *Let It Shine.*

"I've always believed that women should be liberated from anything that restricts them, so back when everybody was burning their bras, I burned my girdle," she told Dolly. Dolly responded, "I would *never* have been so bold as to try to burn my bra. It would have taken the fire department three weeks to put the fire out!''

Oprah mentioned how well Dolly looked, after her dramatic weight loss, and Dolly said, ''Yea, that's all behind me.'' ''For the moment,'' she drawled. The two of them looked stunning together—two true superstars, hand in hand. Backed up by a full chorus and band, the lovely ladies sand *Let It Shine*, the likes of which television has rarely seen, with the audience clapping and singing along. It looked like the entire show might turn into a gospel hour the way the two of them worked up the group.

Oprah doesn't mind appearing alongside other glamorous women like Dolly Parton. She is just as comfortable next to a beautiful fashion model like Ashely Richardson as she is with middle-aged housewives. Oprah has the ability to draw out things from people in such a way that you find yourself in a semi-state of shock. During one of the shows, an elderly lady stood up in the audience. Oprah rushed over to the prim-looking lady and gently extended the microphone. The lady shifted her slight weight, then began: ''My marriage lasted thirty-one years and then came our divorce. I think my husband must have read the Bible once, where it says 'Love thy neighbor','' she said as she stood, clutching a small purse, ''because that's what he did.'' Having gotten that out of her system, the gentle lady went on, ''She was twenty years younger.'' The laughter that rose from hearing about her husband's neighborly lover becomes subdued and the people listen intently. ''She was really like a daughter. Well, after three years, uh, leave them alone and they'll come home, wagging their tails behind him, because that's what he did!''

Not all of her guests have such a pleasant way of looking at things. When Jimmy 'the Weasel' Fratianno, former gangster and Mafia hit man, was a guest on her show, he talked about brutal murders that he committed, beatings, and other Mafia-style activities. Fratianno, fearing that an attack on his life might occur should he appear in the studio, was shown in silhouette on a television monitor. One guest who had experienced numerous attacks and attempts on his life (including a car bombing and two gunshot wounds in the chest) refused to fly to the studio to be on the show; instead he drove hundreds of miles in his own car. Mr. Fratianno didn't want to even take that chance.

"The three people that you strangled," Oprah asked him, "did you find them in bed and strangle them, or did you see them walking down the street and you strangled them?"

The admitted killer answered, "No, no, we did one in my house, and one in another fellow's house in San Diego, and another one in upland California. But we buried them all in the same place. In a vineyard."

"So during this time, this was during what period, when you were a hired contract killer?" Oprah asked. "Well, it was in the fifties," he said, and then claimed that the last time he had killed a person was in 1953. When Oprah asked Fratianno if he felt any remorse or regret about the killings, he responded, "It's just a job."

"Where'd you get the name 'Weasel'," Oprah asks, as if his name was as important as the killings. "Well, that happened when I was about fourteen years old," came the reply. "Where I lived in Cleveland, policemen used to kick us in the butt when we'd steal some fruit. So later on in years, I hit 'em on the face with a tomato; he chased me and couldn't catch me and they said 'Look at Weasel run.' And that's how it stuck on me."

Oprah quickly dropped the subject and proceeded to get to more meaty matters. "When you started talking," she began, referring to Fratianno's habit of informing on his fellow gang members, "having lived within the Family for all of those years, weren't you afraid, knowing the power they had? Weren't you afraid for yourself? Even being protected by the government?"

"Well, after I got into the government," Fratianno said in his rough-sounding voice, "I was kind of leery, you know, if they'd find out where I was at, but before then I was never worried at all."

"Because you hadn't talked?"

"Right."

"So what made you talk?"

"Well, they protected me. There was a contract out on my life and I had two choices. Either go with the government or stay out and get killed."

When Oprah asked Jimmy 'the Weasel' about celebrities who had had a contract out on their life, but hadn't been killed, he bluntly recalled the Desi Arnez tale. "He made *The Untouchables* and he used real names. San Giacanna wanted to kill him. He sent a couple of people out and in the meantime he went to prison and he just forgot about it. From there he went to Mexico."

"Were there other times when you didn't kill people, you just broke a couple of legs?" Oprah asked, trying to get another celebrity story out of him.

"Yes. Well, that was years ago. Jilly Rizzo told me to do something for Frank Sinatra. Somebody talked about him. We went to find him, and the guy was dead."

"And this was because he said something unkind?" Oprah asked.

"Well, he said something about Frank Sinatra in a book that he war writing. We went to look for him and come to find out he was dead."

"But Frank Sinatra didn't tell you to look for him."

"His companion, Jilly Rizzo did. And Frank (Sinatra) even asked me if I'd taken care of it, and I told him, well, we're looking for him, we can't find him."

"Uh, huh," she ssaid thoughtfully. "So he was already dead. Had someone else already gotten to him?"

"Well, no, he died a natural death. I think he died of a heart attack."

"Yea, he heard you were coming," Oprah said as the audience laughed. "And it just killed him!"

On the opposite end of the 'guest-spectrum', Oprah once was talking to a group of four very attractive women who couldn't find dates. Katherine Oxenburg, Blake Carrington's ex-daughter on *Dynasty*, who claimed to have not had a date in over a year; Tracey Ross, model and actress; Stephanie Kramer, star of the TV series *Hunter*; and the young beauty Ashley Richardson, whose face has been seen on the covers of many of the top fashion magazines.

All of the women are very attractive, each with a quality unique to their personalities, yet none of them thought that she was especially pretty. In fact, Stephanie Kramer admitted that she thought she looked "average," and when looking at herself she sees "everything that's wrong before (she) sees what's right." "Ok," Oprah asks, "do you think you are better than average?" Kramer didn't elaborate, simply saying that she really felt she was average. "I'm going to take you to the malls and show you average," Oprah jokes. "Spend a day at the mall, and then you'll know what average is."

Apparently, if you listened to these exceptionally pretty women, and believed what they said about their looks, Oprah Winfrey was the best-looking amongst them.

Ashley Richardson admitted that for a while she thought that she was "dorky-looking." "It's taken five years of modeling," the blonde beauty said as she played with her long hair, "to build up my self-esteem, to realize that I am good-looking, because I never thought I was."

"You have been on the cover of everything that's worth being on the cover of," Oprah smiled. "You're the one Cosmo girl that they didn't have to pump your breasts up!" After a full seven seconds of hearty laughter (Oprah had been right), Oprah piped in, "Helen Gurly (Brown) said, 'Get Ashley, we don't have to pump her up.' " Later on in this program, Ashley Richardson said that she had never been asked out on a date. With her looks, and the exposure from *The Oprah Winfrey Show*, you can bet that by the time you read this, she's been asked.

Katherine Oxenburg told Oprah that she's too shy to date, and that on a usual Saturday night she stays home and reads. "The last attempt at a date," the British actress laughs, "I had an argument with a guy on the phone because he was pissed off that I would never call him. 'Well, I'm old-fashioned' " she told him, "and it's up to the man to call, and that's the way I am. It's very difficult."

"When you look in the mirror, do you see what we see?" Oprah asked her. "Before or after I've put on my makeup?" "Before *and* after," Oprah chimes in. "Before, I've heard you say that you look like you're twelve."

"Yea, pretty much. I look like a little kid. I don't feel particularly beautiful. I don't look at myself in the mirror and say, 'This is a beautiful woman.' "

"So if you don't think you're beautiful, who do you think is?" Oprah asks her.

"Oh God!" Oxenburg laments. "There's so many. I mean there's Michelle Pfeiffer; there is a list of girls I'd like to look like."

Never one to leave any stone unturned, Oprah shoots, "Continue the list."

"Continue the list? Kim Bassinger, Katherine Deneuve, it goes on, believe me."

"OK," Oprah says, not letting up, "Let's get . . . truthful here. When you look at yourself, don't you think, 'Well . . . I'm pretty good.'?"

"Only when I look in here," Oxenburg says as she pats her girlishly small chest. "It's not my face. If I'm feeling good about myself, virtually, then I feel beautiful."

"That's the kind of comment I expected you to say," Oprah kids.

The second half of the program showed the male 'can't get a date' perspective. Oprah invited four handsome young men to share their thoughts and feelings on the subject, and even though they tried, it was difficult foro them. Two of the four men, caught up with everyone knowing that they hadn't had a date for some time, went ahead and asked the ladies for dates while on the air. None of the men asked Oprah for a date; they probably understood that her intimate times are spent with Stedman Graham. In fact, wedding plans have been rumored and they apparently have a December wedding planned.

Will Stedman Graham be the future husband of America's favorite talk-show gal? Will Oprah finlly get to raise children of her own? Only time will tell. In the meantime, we must be happy that they've found each other, and that they love each other. True love has been a long time coming for them both, and they deserve each other's happiness.

With enormous popularity sometimes comes a slew of rumors and excessive innuendos. At times it's extremely difficult to find out about our 'stars'. Because they're in the public eye so much, they're not exactly quick to tell about a personal or private event when it occurs. There are the ever-present tabloids, and scandal-sheet-style newspapers, who never miss a chance to report whatever they can find out (or invent) about them.

Take, for instance, the future wedding plans of Oprah Winfrey and Stedman Graham. Not content to wait and find out from Oprah about her relationship with Graham, one tabloid 'invented' the story of its demise. The rotten thing about these scandal sheets is that the people who read them only do so to find out more about their favorite stars. They aren't necessarily looking for dirty gossip about their favorites. Instead, they look to find information about them. The erroneous reports do nothing but harm the subjects of these cruel methods of selling newspapers.

The readers are often too smart for the articles, though. They see right through the lies and think for themselves. One woman who has had it with this kind of reporting wrote this letter to Ann Landers: "Dear Ann: I read an article recently in a supermarket scandal sheet that bothered me a lot. It was about one of my favorite people, Oprah Winfrey. The story said that she had been jilted by her fiancé, Stedman Graham, a handsome ex-college football player, and that the Christmas wedding plans were off. There were a lot of details about how Oprah was shattered and bitter, crying her heart out between segments of her TV show. It said that even though she presents a smiling face to her public, her heart is broken."

"A few days after I read the article I happened to see Oprah and her friend on Michigan Avenue. They were laughing and having a good time. She surely didn't look shattered and bitter, like a woman who was crying her heart out. I gathered my courage and called my cousin who knows one of Oprah's staff people. I just had to know if that story was true. The reply was, as I expected, that it was totally false. There wasn't a shred of truth to it. To put it bluntly, it was a damn lie."

"Will you please tell me, Ann, how can a publication get away with printing 'damn lies'? Why don't the people who are muddied up by these awful papers sue them?"

"I am eager to read your answer in the paper." The letter was signed, "Steamed in Chicago."

Ann Landers was quick to point out many of the reasons the smear mags are getting away with the unsubstantiated things that they print. "Dear Steamed: There are some very good reasons for not suing a sleazy sheet for printing 'damned lies'."

"First: When the story of the suit appears, the lies are repeated and a great many people who didn't hear them the first time around are suddenly informed. All the while, the sleaze sheet thrives on the publicity."

"Second: Each time a motion is filed or another action is taken in court, the story is retold. Lawyers defending the paper have been known to file ridiculous motions just to get additional publicity."

"Third: The party doing the suing must prove that his or her earnings have been damaged by the bad publicity, and this is often extremely difficult. Once the question of damages is brought up, the attorneys for the scandal sheet have the right to cross-examine the suing party about contracts, earnings, net worth, etc. All the information is made public."

"Fourth: Lawsuits can be enormously expensive and time-consuming. A busy person may be forced to spend days, weeks, or months tied up in litigation. A long, drawn-out trial can cost a fortune."

"Fifth: The chances of collecting significant money from a sleaze sheet in the case of a favorable verdict are often slim. Some publications hide their assets by resorting to a variety of gimmicks, and as the saying goes, you can't get blood out of a turnip."

"Unfortunately, these miserable little rags that feed on sensationalism will continue to publish gross distortions and 'damned lies' because the attorneys for celebrities are well aware of the facts that I have just outlined."

Ms. Landers summed up her thoughts by saying, "Unfair? You better believe it. The moral of the story is: Don't accept as fact everything you read. It ain't necessarily so."

True, Oprah hasn't been immune to vicious and scandalous lies in the tabloid-style newspapers; no celebrity is. She does tend to rise above it all, and come out of these kinds of scrapes triumphant. She doesn't really let the articles get her down, though they are a constant nuisance. One popular joke is that all of the celebrities who get mentioned or lied about in the tabloids should get together and make a newspaper of their own, where they can make up wild, imaginative stories about the owners and editors of the existing ones (the problem with that being, no-one would bother to read it).

7

Dollars and Steds

"When you pay cash for stuff, you don't have to fill out any forms. You don't have to wait for management approval. You don't give out references, your previous address. This is the life."

—OPRAH WINFREY

Oprah Winfrey is rich beyond her wildest dreams. Anything she wants, she can buy. Wherever she wants to go, she can go. Whatever she might need, she has only to ask and she can have it. She recently decided to reward her father for all that he'd done for her. She told Joan Barthel, "I called up my father and said, 'Dad, I'm a millionaire! I want to send you and your friends to any place in the world you want to go.' And he said, 'All I want is some new tires for my truck.' I was so upset!" Oprah's mother, however, wasn't as reluctant to accept a gift from her millionaire daughter. "I don't feel I owe anybody anything. But my mother feels I do, so I bought her a house in Milwaukee. Maybe I feel guilty because I'm such an independent being. I'm hearing from so many people now who want me to give them money or lend them money. I say I'll give you the shirt off my back as long as you don't ask me for it.''

Oprah loves to spend her hard-earned money on fine furs, designer clothes, and lavish gifts. The stunning gown that she wore to the 1986 Oscars ceremony was designed by the renowned Bob Mackie and cost her a cool $10,000. When she arrived at the New York premiere of Steven Spielberg's *The Color Purple,* she wowed the crowds with a bright, purple-dyed $10,000 fur. She even gives expensive furs to her friends and family as presents.

Oprah moved into her sprawling high-rise apartment in Chicago's exclusive Gold Coast area in 1986. The apartment, on the 57th floor of the building, is decorated with such luxurious items as a marble bathtub with gold fixtures. She even claims to have what she calls "crystal chandeliers lighting up the inside of (her) closets." Her towering view is spectacular, giving her a full vista of Chicago and the brisk waters of Lake Michigan.

The same year Oprah moved into her luxury condominium, she met Stedman Graham. The two had met many times at charitable functions, such as the Athletes Against Drugs organization, which is headed by Graham. With each meeting, the two seemed to grow closer and more casual, until they finally went out together on a dinner date. Oprah was reluctant, at first, to involve herself in a serious relationship. She kept telling herself to take things slowly and wait to see what happens.

Not long before Oprah Winfrey and Stedman Graham were considered a hot item, Oprah told Chris Anderson about sharing her personal life with a man and a double career. "Hard? Make that impossible." Oprah hadn't had a steady relationship since she had left Baltimore. She said, "I learned that you can't change other people. Only yourself." Her needs at that time were "that a man be tall, that he have his own money, and that he be spiritually grounded."

She told Audrey Edwards that, at that time, she wasn't

actively pursuing a long-term relationship, saying that she
didn't "even have a goldfish." "I would love to have a
significant other in my life," she told Edwards. "That
would be wonderful," she wished. "But everything in life
is about timing, and obviously the timing's not right for
me now." It wasn't long after she said these things that
she and Graham were on their way to a long-awaited,
mutually compatible relationship.

Oprah talked to her audience about the difficulties of
secretly man-hunting. "This is what we've heard, 'You
just really need to stop looking and putting pressure on it.'
I've been told that 'the minute you stop looking you will
find him.' I've gone to many a banquet I didn't want to go
to because I thought, 'Maybe he'll be here.' You walk into
the room and say 'Okay, God, I'm not looking, but . . . ?' "

Once on *The Late Show*, while Joan Rivers was the
host, Oprah talked about her man, Graham. "He's six feet
six of terrific!" she said to Joan. When Rivers offered to
let Stedman Graham come on stage with her and Oprah, he
'Stedfastly' refused. He just didn't want to share Oprah's
spotlight. Oprah told Joan, "He's so private . . . I knew
he wouldn't, and I respect that. Usually, you get guys
when you're a high profile who walk into a room and
they're looking for a camera."

When the subject of weight was brought up by Joan
(both Oprah and Joan Rivers are equally adept at getting
right to the point), Oprah said, "I've reached a point in
my life now where I think it's OK. I'm going to lose it.
And you know what? The slower you lose it," she offered, "the better. You know when you pig out and you
fast and you pig out? You drop ten pounds in four days
and it's back by the fifth? I'm done with that," she
kidded. Joan suggested to Oprah that she looked much
slimmer since she had been seeing Stedman Graham. Oprah
let out a wry smile and said, "It's helpful because he has
such a great body." Oprah said in *Ebony* that Graham is
"an overwhelmingly decent man. He has made me realize

a lot of the things that were missing in my life, like the sharing that goes on between two people.''

It might be difficult for some to imagine that someone as independent and rich as Oprah would need a man in her life. Her wealth isn't just her money, however; Oprah's fortune lies in the diversity of her interests. Stedman Graham is another interlocking puzzle piece that helps complete the picture of Oprah Winfrey. Though fame, fortune, and Stedman Graham are each significant parts of her life, she enjoys them all to the best of her abilities.

Fourteen years ago, Oprah was a young radio announcer at a small black radio station. Today she lives in an $800,000 condominium, drives a flashy, imported automobile, and dresses in the most expensive clothes money can buy; yet she is the same young woman who almost took her own life only a few years ago. The sharing, compassionate, generous human being that you see on television is the same person that only a few get to see in her less public activities.

Oprah's generosity knows no bounds. One day she'll buy a house for her mother, the next she'll buy a car for a friend. Just recently, it was reported in *Forbes* that she bought a new Jaguar Xj-S for her lawyer/manager, Jeff Jacobs (the fellow who runs Oprah's production company, Harpo Inc., along with her cousin Jo); a new Volkswagon for her assistant; and an Oldsmobile for Graham's mother's birthday after she turned an incredible 100 years old. How can she spend so much on other people and still keep plenty for herself? That's easy. She makes more money than she knows what to do with. An article in *Variety* reported that by their estimate, Oprah's earnings would exceed $31 million dollars, more than Bill Cosby or Johnny Carson. The article said that *The Oprah Winfrey Show* would earn King World $125 million, and that she would be making an unconfirmed 25% of the gross. *Forbes* reported a much lesser earnings estimate, saying that she will make $8 million dollars per year. In an anonymous figure published in *Parade Magazine*, it was reported that "at this point, Oprah's show is carried by 135 stations, and she's in demand. But estimates of her fortune are highly exaggerated." The magazine went on to say that "she's worth between $3 million and $4 million" dollars.

According to the article in *Forbes*, Oprah has been protecting her income by establishing a "personal investment committee, consisting of her lawyer/manager Jeff Jacobs, a tax accountant from Price Waterhouse, two trust officers from Harris Bank, two money manager-brokers from Goldman Sachs, and a bond portfolio manager from Exchange National Bank which meets every six weeks or so. They put her in a mixture of stocks, tax-free bonds and other properties."

When Oprah feels like dabbling in the market, on her own, she uses the same common sense that she's used to get where she is today. She said in *Forbes*, "I bought Reebok because everywhere I walked, I saw people wearing Reeboks." Later, when the price of Reebok stock went up, up, up, Oprah sold and earned $110 profit per share.

With all that money, and all those assistants and money managers to pay, you might think Oprah would get 'lofty' and start throwing her weight around to ensure getting her way. Not so. She can't even bring herself to ride in a limousine (though recently she bought a silver Mercedes limo). She did for a while, but she just wasn't comfortable being driven around for longer than two weeks. She felt like she was "taking up (the driver's) time". Now she drives herself in her striking ocean-blue Jaguar Xj-S. There's a big difference between riding quietly in the back of a limousine and gliding through the streets of Chicago with the top down and the music up.

When talking to *Forbes*, Oprah said that she was just beginning to realize how great it is to have lots and lots of money. "Did you know," Oprah said, "when you pay cash for stuff, you don't have to fill out any forms? You don't have to wait for management approval. You don't have to give out references, your previous address." Oprah rounded out her feelings about being a multi-millionaire by saying, "This is the life!"

For now, Oprah does her best to hold on to all she's accumulated by limiting her personal spending to a mere $1 million dollars per year. Though her generosity and acting activities, along with the company of Stedman Graham, are enough to keep Oprah happy for some time, she still has a few things to wish for. One is to own a sprawling ranch of her own, in Santa Fe, New Mexico, as soon as she can arrange it. Someday soon, Stedman Graham and Oprah Winfrey may be enacting their own version of The American Gothic as they watch the warm summer clouds roll by, and sit on the porch whittling out the head of a small corncob doll. Nah! Who would cook the roast beef?

To prepare for her starring role in *The Women of Brewster Place*, Oprah agreed to do her best to shed as many pounds as possible, with a goal set at a whopping fifty pounds. Oprah has been trying for years to leave her excess weight behind, and now it seems that the 5-foot, seven-inch-tall woman will come very close to her youthful weight. She has taken every measure to stick to a strict daily plan by hiring a special cook who prepares delicious low-calorie meals and dietetic snacks for her. She really means to lose the weight for the role. She said in the *Ladies Home Journal* that diets don't work for her. "I've gained seventy pounds since I first started dieting."

"I'm determined; this time I'm going to lose fifty pounds and keep them off." Oprah said of her lightly prepared meals and daily aerobic conditioning, "I will never diet again." At the time the *Ladies Home Journal* article was being written, Oprah had already lost a load-lightening twenty pounds.

Oprah attributes some of her interest in a swiftly executed weight loss to *The Women of Brewster Place*, and also to Stedman Graham. Though the pair won't publicly admit to a yearning for marriage, the rumors and wedding talk abound. Recently Oprah said in a brief article in *US* magazine, "Honey, if I wanted a wedding dress, you know Bob Mackie would design it." She denied that she would buy a dress off of the rack; then she denied that she was even engaged to be married. Oprah is still Oprahistic about the possibilities of a future marriage, though. "I don't want to make any predictions about marriage just yet," she said. "But yet, I'm in love and it's a wonderful feeling. The success of my show is great, but nothing compares with being in love. Zippity-doodah," she smiles, "I'm in love."

"He's so handsome," Oprah said admiringly. "Oooh, what a body, so I figured, if he's calling me, he's either a jerk or there's something wrong with him I should know about." As it turns out, Graham was neither nor both. He just happened to be an attractive, muscular man who liked what he saw in Oprah Winfrey. "He's as kind as he is tall," Oprah proudly announced. "He's my number-one fan, and he isn't jealous of my success. In a relationship where one person is always in the public eye, it can be hard for the other person—particularly if it's a man—to be able to stand back and say, 'Okay, you go for it if you want to.' But he can, and that means a lot to me."

Oprah told the *Journal* that in public, she and Stedman Graham are approached constantly. People want to sit and have lunch with them when they come across them in a restaurant, or they just come up to the pair on the streets. "I was having dinner with Stedman at a restaurant recently, and a woman at a nearby table recognized me and came over to chat. Then she called her husband over and they helped themselves to our chairs. When the waiter came, they ordered some dessert. Guess who had to pick up the bill?"

Still, unannounced visits with overexuberant fans are just a small part of Oprah's daily activities as a superstar performer. "Right now," Oprah said in the *Ladies Home Journal*, "I feel about as good as you can feel."

Thirty-six-year-old Stedman Graham, the executive director of the Athletes Against Drugs organization, has been seeing Oprah long enough to know that as a companion to a superstar, public appearances are no family picnic. Often portrayed as a scowling chaperone in magazine layouts, Graham is really a kind-hearted man who likes to look after his relationship with Oprah.

Graham agreed to say a few words about his feelings as the mate of America's fastest rising personality. He told Julie Chenault, "The most difficult thing to deal with when you're dating the 'hottest star in the country' is that you're surrounded by people all the time. You really have no privacy. But you have to try to keep things in perspective. It takes a patience to last in this kind of situation. You need to be disciplined, and it helps to be somewhat secure about yourself. I feel that I don't have to be with her just to ego-trip. I believe I get enough attention on my own merits—that's sufficient for me."

"Because of the position she's in, a lot of people look at my involvement with her in terms of what they feel I'm taking from her, not what I may be giving to her. They don't realize that I need certain things from a relationship, just as she does."

Finally, we get to hear his side of the story; for so long he's been the silent partner. Standing almost a full foot above Oprah's demure 5-foot, seven-inch frame, Stedman's appearance commands attention, whether he's with Oprah or without. But the two of them could draw stares at a convention of the near-sighted.

"I try to spend as much time as I can with Oprah. But the amount of time really depends a lot on her schedule. With things going for her the way they are now, most of the flexibility has to come from my end. If I didn't have my own business and work for myself, then it would be almost impossible for the relationship to exist."

"Because of our relationship," Graham said, "I don't think of Oprah as a star. But she is a strong personality. She wants to do what she wants to do, and I want to do what I want to do. We don't have arguments, but rather discussions—I don't like to argue. We both do a lot of compromising."

"In *Essence,* Stedman Graham calmly revealed the thoughts he has about Oprah's increasing popularity, "The interesting thing about dating someone who's in the limelight is that you take on the same importance that they do. But the reverse is also true. For instance, if she gets into a situation and does something wrong and the public suddenly goes against her, then I've got to deal with that, too. On the other hand, opportunities are often available for me that I wouldn't have if I were not associated with Oprah. My ideas have greater scope now, and I feel she's responsible for a lot of the growth I've made since we've been together. I think that she's also grown a lot. I hope she has, and I feel that I'm partially responsible for it. I always encourage her to be the best that she can possibly be. If we can no longer grow together, then we need to reexamine our relationship."

Susan Taylor once asked Oprah what she thought was so special about Stedman Graham. "The greatest thing about him," Oprah said, "is his kindness. And he knows who he is. I am thrilled that I have discovered this in a Black man."

Oprah won't readily admit that she and Graham have set a wedding date, or that she wants to marry him. "I don't know," she said thoughtfully. "I think I'd like to marry him, because I don't think I'll find a person of greater character. If I were going to marry someone, I'd like someone like Stedman."

Probably the most difficult things Oprah and Stedman have to share in their relationship are the never-ending string of rumors. Oprah does this, Stedman does that. They have been learning to cope, however, with the gossip and wild talk. "We're both getting tougher skins. He gets more upset than I do about people's false claims about why he's with me."

"Do people suggest that it's because you have money and you're on television?" Ms. Taylor asked her. "Of course,'' Oprah responds, ''and one of the reasons they say that is because he's so good-looking. If he didn't look the way he does, I'm sure there would not be as many rumors. People naturally assume that he couldn't really care for me. For that same reason *I* thought he wouldn't be interested in me. So other women, in order to make themselves feel good and to rationalize why they don't have this type of man, say 'It has to be the fame. It certainly couldn't be just for herself, because she looks like *me*. If that's the case, then I should be able to get him.' ''

''Stedman and I met in Chicago,'' Oprah remembers. ''We attended some of the same functions. At the time he was dating someone else and was loyal to her. Thank goodness that's the kind of man he is. If he's dating someone, he doesn't show interest in another woman. I appreciate that quality. So I knew him as an attached man, and there were never any sparks.''

''After his relationship ended, he asked me out a couple of times. At first I wasn't really that interested because, for one, I still had doubts about myself. He's a very attractive man. And I was thinking, *'That kind of man usually goes for cupcakes.'* Vanilla-cream cupcakes. One of those women with long hair who has had her nose done, or was born with her nose that way. And those women have real green eyes, not contacts. So that's what I thought. I still have this poor self-image. So I ignored him, thinking, 'I don't know what he's calling *me* for.' Actually, he called three times over a period of time. The first time I stood him up. The second time I made excuses, and it was all because of my insecurities. Finally, the third time, he said, 'I'm not going to ask you anymore.' So I went out with him. On the way to the theater he stopped and bought me flowers from someone selling them on the street. I thought, 'Now what's he doing? He got me flowers.' It had been a long time since I'd been treated kindly by a man.''

8

A Spiritual Understanding

"I ask that I be able to live my life so that it magnifies the power of God that is in me. I need to get to the point where I have as much love in my heart for other people as I should have. And I'm striving for wisdom, truth, and love."

—OPRAH WINFREY

Oprah keeps her eyes on her past so that she can better live her adult life. The curses and torture that she endured as a child, and the lack of motherly love or a family atmosphere, are a cold memory that Oprah chooses not to forget. Instead, she uses these experiences to make her life more livable. And with her belief in God firmly in check, she humbly accepts what 'She' has in store for her. Prayer and silent communion are as much a part of Oprah's life as her television show, her movies, and Stedman Graham. She reads that Bible every day; she even has one in her office, at WLS-TV in Chicago, where she tapes *The Oprah Winfrey Show*. She attends church regularly and often in the company of Stedman Graham. The spiritual beliefs that she shares with Graham and her viewers are not of the 'Repent or Die' type, nor are they the long-winded 'preachy' kind either. She uses the Bible as a source of inspiration, and her silent beliefs are never aimed at anyone in particular except herself. Her relationship with God is as it should be. It is with God and Oprah.

And does God watch over and protect Oprah? "Sometimes She does!", Oprah laughs. During her first six years with Hattie Mae Lee, her grandmother, Oprah's life was a mixture of pleasure and pain, yet it was at this time, she claims, that her first introduction to a spiritual understanding occurred. "It was lonely," Oprah told Leslie Rubinstein about her time with Hattie Mae. "I had one corncob doll," she sadly recalls. "I rode a pig bareback and spent most of my time reading Bible stories to the barnyard animals."

"I remember when I was four, watching my grandma boil clothes in a huge iron pot," Oprah remembers clearly. "I was crying and Grandma asked, 'What's the matter with you, girl?' 'Big Mammy,' I sobbed, 'I'm going to die someday.' 'Honey,' she said, 'God doesn't mess with His children. You gotta do a lot of work in your life and not be afraid. The strong have got to take care of the others.' "

Not all of her grandmother's lessons were painful ones, apparently. When Oprah talks about her grandmother, she mentions the cruelties, but she also talks about the inspiration that her grandmother set forth in her mind as a young girl. "I soon came to realize that my Grandma was loosely translating from the Epistle to the Romans in the New Testament: 'We that are strong ought to bear the infirmities of the weak.' Despite my age, I somehow grasped the concept. I knew I was going to help people, that I had a higher calling, so to speak."

"Sure, Grandma whipped me, she sure did. But she taught me about life, and I loved her so. I'll look like her when I'm old," Oprah admitted. "I'll be one of those spiritual ladies rock'n and shout'n in church. Yes, ma'am, you'll find me in the amen corner."

Oprah attributes her strong feelings, firm convictions, and sense of honest confidence to her past. The experiences that discouraged her in the past are what makes her so strong today. She said to Susan Taylor, "I think it just comes from living and taking notes while I'm living; appreciating the mistakes I've made, and looking at them as part of my growth. I also think a lot of it is background. You know, as Black people, we all share the same kind of emotional roots. Spending the first six years of my life with my grandmother (in the South) instilled a kind of strength and a belief system in me that I didn't know I had. But I am where I am because I believed in my possibilities. Everything in your world is created by what you think."

Oprah's strong beliefs in herself are only possible because of her belief in God and her constant struggle to fulfill her farthest potential by giving her service to others. She wouldn't be enjoying her wealth and fame if she couldn't give of herself to the people she's able to help. That is why she gives so much of herself, in order to stay happy. The old adage 'It is better to give than to receive' is transformed into 'Oprah must give, in order to feel good about what she receives.'

When Oprah was scheduled to attend the Academy Awards ceremony, she had designer Bob Mackie create her stunning $10,000 gown. But when the time came to put on the dress and drive to the ceremony, she found to her aggravation that the dress didn't fit. In fact, it was so small that it took three people to squeeze her into the expensive garment as she lay on the floor struggling along with them. She finally managed to squeeze herself into the thing, but had to lay down in the limousine on the way to the gala affair. She had the driver stop at a distance from the event, and she and her assistants walked the remaining way so that no one saw her being pushed to her feet. An amusing tale, yes, but at the time Oprah was not amused. Whenever the applause at the awards ceremony brought people to their feet, she had to be helped up so that she didn't rip right through the tight-fitting dress. Today, she is able to get a mild chuckle out of the tale, as few women could. Most would never reveal the trying time; the embarrassment would be too much. "I traveled to the Oscars on my back," Oprah relates, "in the back of the limousine. How to get out? I asked the driver to stop a block before the theater and I rolled out. I sat in the gown all night and couldn't breathe!"

Oprah had really expected to win an Oscar that night, or she might not have been so nervous beforehand as she was. She was tortured with the possibility of receiving such a tremendous award and let the prospect get to her. After all, *The Color Purple* received ten Academy Award nominations, but when it came time to award the Oscars, the film was practically ignored. "I was stunned," Oprah admits. "It was the worst night of my life." When she returned to her hotel room after the depressing ceremony, she was literally scissored out of her expensive gown.

"I didn't win an Oscar," Oprah sadly recalled in a conversation with Leslie Rubinstein. "Perhaps God was saying to me, 'Oprah, you are not winning because your dress is too tight for you to make it up all those steps to receive your statuette.' "

The more Oprah does, the more she learns. Though there will always be problems for her, she still has things that go her way. Having been too short on credits in college, Oprah didn't have an actual diploma until recently. One was awarded to her from Tennessee State University last May. In the company of her father, Oprah gave a 'stirring' commencement address to the graduating students and faculty. Vernon Winfrey says that Oprah's appearance caused quite a stir at his Nashville barber shop as well as at the commencement ceremony. He told Leslie Rubinstein, "The best thing about Oprah's being famous is to let young folks know she came from a poor family." Vernon's life hasn't really changed much with Oprah's popularity. "Oprah's offered me all these gifts," he says, "but I don't need anything, except maybe a better TV at the shop so I can watch her show."

As well as Oprah and her father seem to be getting along recently, she still has a problem dealing with her mother's attitude about her fortunate success. Vernita Lee apparently feels that Oprah owes her for the time she spent with her as a child, saying that "there are dues to pay." Instead of becoming agitated or angry, Oprah turns her cheek and spends a small fortune keeping her mother happy. "This doesn't solve all those years of my feeling unloved," Oprah testifies, "but my mother did the most she could. When I'm feeling real bad, I put on Aretha Franklin's album *Amazing Grace!* and I grab my Bible. I ask myself, 'Oprah, are you going to be a victim, or are you going to take charge of your life?' And when I'm in control, I feel like soaring over mountains. I move with the flow and take life's curves, letting the universe handle the details. I know exactly where I'm going. And God's right beside me all the way."

When Oprah was sixteen she was voted the most popular girl in her class. (Her campaign slogan was 'Grand Ole Oprah'.) And if there was such an award today, she would probably win the same title again. In a recent letter from a reader of *Good Housekeeping*, a woman from Othello, Washington, Annette Roberts, wrote: "Thank you for sharing Oprah (August) with your readers. It was one of the most interesting articles I've read in some time. Oprah Winfrey has proven what a person can achieve if she's determined. She deserves all of her success."

Part of the success Oprah has achieved is due to her inquisitive interest in the human condition. Her interview with the little girl in Midland, Texas, will no doubt raise her popularity in all parts of the country, but especially in Midland. I know from first-hand experience, having spent many weeks in the black ghettos of Midland's outskirts, that the people there treat you with much kindness and respect, and that Oprah's journey there will magnify her reputation as a loving and caring person. Not only the black community there welcomed Oprah, but all the people of Midland, Texas, who have a style and warmth of their own. Having Oprah there will bring more light to their city. The surrounding area is often golden-brown in color, and somewhat dusty, with oil wells, small and large, spreading over the countryside. There are so many oil wells that it was only a matter of time before something happened to make people aware of their danger. It is a miracle that the result wasn't Jessica's death.

"People see me on television," Oprah says of herself, "and read about me in newspapers. But that isn't who I am—that's what I do. I am just a woman striving. Striving to magnify the Lord. That's all." . . . "I ask that I be able to live my life so that it magnifies the power of God that is in me. I need to get to the point where I have as much love in my heart for other people as I should have. And I'm striving for wisdom, truth, and love."

Oprah takes time out of every day to commune with the Lord. She reads the Bible and listens to rousing gospel music on her radio every morning. "Today I read from the New Testament Epistle to the Ephesians," Oprah says proudly. "One God and father of all, who is above all, and through all, and in you all. I call my morning ritual 'centering up'. At night I get on my knees and pray. I feel incomplete without it." Stedman Graham, who used to play basketball for Hardin-Simmons and holds a graduate degree in education, prays too. "Stedman also prays on his knees," Oprah reveals, "every night." The pair also attend the same Baptist church together on Sunday mornings.

"I think the best thing about being where I am and who I am, right now," Oprah says, "is that I am spiritually comfortable with all of it. I see it as a blessing, a bonus for doing work that I really love to do. And the best part of it is that I have no fear of losing it, or fear of what tomorrow holds for me. I know God holds the future. Also I feel spiritually grounded and secure. And so the benefits are that much greater."

Susan L. Taylor asked Oprah, "You, like everyone,

have had joy and pain in your life. When you spoke on your show some time ago of having been sexually abused as a child, was that the first time you'd acknowledged it?'' Oprah responded, ''It was certainly the first time I'd publicly acknowledged it. And in retrospect I probably would not have chosen to do it that way. We were doing a show of women who were sexually abused, and I was caught up in empathizing with with women there. There was an entire audience of them. For so long you carry this burden, and you believe it's your fault. I realize a lot of people felt I was being exploitative. Many people who don't understand sexual abuse ask, 'Why are they talking about it on television? And why is she asking that woman to tell what her father did in explicit detail?' ''

''The reason I said 'this happened to me too' is so that people would not think that I was just getting off on this girl talking about what had happened to her. Another reason is that people can look at one guest from a small town in Missouri and say, 'Well, yeah, that's her, but it doesn't really happen.' Although I probably wouldn't have chosen that way to share it, it has certainly done a lot of good for a lot of people.''

''At this point in my life I really do have it all. And when I pray I don't ask for anything, except glory and greatness. What I know is that greatness isn't determined by how many people know you—it's determined by service to other people.''

Still, Oprah wants to be liked as much as anyone else does. She really feels badly when people miss the true side of her personality, never seeing the real person that she is inside. It is not the exclusive fault of the viewers who think badly of her; television has used every trick up its sleeve to lure potential viewers. TV has lied, cheated, and literally fooled people in the past, and TV will fool them again in the future. It's a good thing, though, that Oprah has come to us in the disillusioned age that she has. ''I live my life and I do this show to try to raise people's consciousness, to give people a sense of hope in their lives.

So when people write or say negative things . . . about me, it really upsets me, because it means that they don't understand me or what my show is about. They've missed it. But I'm convinced that if people who believe that really got to know me, they wouldn't think I was that kind of person.''

"As long as you have the power to bow your head and bend your knees, you do it and God will hear you better.'' Oprah's grandmother's words ring true to the heart, and she remembers them and abides by them.

9

The Final Chapter

Here's to the maiden of bashful fifteen
  Here's to the widow of fifty
Here's to the flaunting, extravagant queen:
  And here's to the housewife that's thirty.

—R. B. SHERIDAN

Oprah's face is seen in magazines and newspapers across this country almost daily. She is recognized wherever she happens to be, and fans cluster themselves around her whenever they get the chance. Her popularity has risen to such highs that even in a tremendously large crowd, she is noticed almost immediately.

A recent example was at the Rosemont Horizon Arena in Chicago. Scheduled to perform here is the music world's own Lionel Richie, one of the top pop performers today. But at one point this night, the famous singer was overshadowed by another famous star: Oprah Winfrey. As people started to notice that Oprah was with them in the sell-out audience, they momentarily forgot Lionel Richie and began a chant of recognition to her. "Oprah! Oprah! Oprah!" they chanted. The audience stood on chairs to get a better look; they shouted and called to her. They cheered and waved. The people did everything short of throwing babies into the air. The appreciative chanting increased and rose above the audience, causing the semi-reluctant Oprah to get up on her chair and greet the mass of people with a pearly grin and gleeful wave of her arms. As she waved mightily, the huge crowd erupted into a full minute-long accolade of hoots, hollers, cheers, and applause. Then came a newer chant: "We love you, Oprah! We love you, Oprah!" The massive audience bombarded her with love and praise. Just fifteen short minutes before the curtain rises and pop superstar Lionel Richie will perform, a short, slightly overweight black woman is getting more attention that the star who is about to appear on stage.

It is true that Oprah is a modern entertainment phenomenon. She doesn't, however, let the popularity blind her to the basic facts of reality. She still sees things in a modest light and does her best to enjoy what she's accomplished in her scant 33 years. She doesn't always give herself full credit when discussing her achievements. If anything, she downplays them. Her incredible life story has been told so many different times that sometimes she even wonders if it doesn't all sound a little trite by now.

Well, to Oprah her life may seem like a kind of cliché, but to her millions of adoring fans, every little incident from her past is an important slice of her life's pie. Every detail available is wanted, good or bad. Though the good details are more plentiful than the bad ones, she does her best to tell it like it is. As she's said many times, "Let's be honest," and that's just what she is. She is 28 years away from the warm-bottomed days of her youth, when she used to sit on her grandmother's dusty porch and read from the Bible.

Most people who get to know her, whether personally or from her television broadcasts, like her. Leslie Rubinstein called her "the queen of television talk, with the friendli-

est brown eyes since Lassie." She went on to say, "The
former shy girl from Kosciusko, Mississippi, who didn't
wear shoes until she was six, now wears pricy lizard (skin)
cowboy boots with mink." America loves a success story.
There is little doubt about that. But for some reason,
Oprah has captured the hearts of millions with her pres-
ence and will do just that for quite some time. Her recol-
lections of past events are clear and vivid, and she doesn't
mind sharing a little fun with her viewers.

Some folks call her Oopy, Ofra, Okrah, Opel Rinky,
Opera, Okla Wintry, and even Opal Winkey. The mere
fact that so many people have been thinking enough about
her to come up with funny names is a small tribute in
itself, and Oprah enjoys sharing the laugh. They are also a
small part of her growing legend.

"Since her show went national, Oprah has been so
successful," says Leslie Rubinstein, "she has become a
household word. She has turned a disturbed childhood into
a rags-to-riches success story. Oprah reputedly earns more
money than Johnny Carson ($20 million). According to
Variety, Winfrey's personal take of the show's profits
slated to reach $125 million in the 1987–88 season could
be $31 million." "I knew I'd be a millionaire by age 32,"
Oprah grins. "In fact I am going to be the richest black
woman in America."

"Meanwhile," reports Rubinstein, "Winfrey spends her
money freely. Recently she gave her producer, Debbie
DiMaio, a six-carat diamond bracelet; the card read, "Brilliance deserves brilliance." Not long ago she handed another staffer the keys to a snazzy convertible, sent two
others to Switzerland on holiday, and recently joined three
of them at the Rancho La Puerta health spa in Mexico."

"At the Academy Awards ceremony she was photographed with the likes of Goldie Hawn, Kathleen Turner,
Sigourney Weaver, and Shirley MacLean. She wore a
beaded black silk dress and according to one gossip tabloid, she stole the show. And last June, she hosted the
Daytime Emmy Awards."

No story can be complete without all of the details. That is undisputable. It would be one thing to mention Oprah's black $10,000 designer gown, but without knowing about her squirming around in the back of the limousine, it's just an expensive dress. The tale would be incomplete. There were many years that Oprah couldn't even afford a dress, and had to wear the roughly sewn ones that 'Big Mammy' made for her by hand. Now she can spend thousands of dollars on them and it barely makes a dent in her savings.

She has recently started to use her incredible reserves of money to buy expensive fashion accessories. Take, for instance, her newest fashion addition: green contact lenses. When asked if her green contacts were a 'negation of her blackness', Oprah responded, "I have just started doing this. I've worn contact lenses since I was 17 years old, and this is the same as changing the color of my pantyhose to me. It's not because I want to be white. About two years ago I was thinking about having my nose done, and I decided not to because I thought, 'God has blessed me with this nose and I've been able to do okay with it.' I haven't given much thought to green contacts. But I guess that's something else to get complaints about. I look at it as purely cosmetic. It's not a statement about me wanting to be white."

Oprah is used to the intense pressures of negative comments and unsavory disclosures, though sometimes it is difficult for her to take them all in stride. They leave a lasting impression; she is a sensitive person and the comments affect her. For example, the abuse she received from her peers as a student left such an impression on her that she thinks about them even today. She wishes that she could have handled them better. It is the same with the criticism that she receives today. "I don't handle it as well as I should," Oprah says reluctantly. "I say, 'It's okay, it doesn't bother me, it comes with the territory,' but then I internalize it and say, 'Okay, now what did I do to create that, and why do they feel that way and what am I doing wrong?' I don't mind criticism if it's justified. What disturbs me about that kind of criticism is that people miss what I am trying to give, or what I am trying to be.''

"I know and understand that I am where I am because of the bridges that I crossed to get here. Sojourner Truth was a bridge. Harriet Tubman was a bridge. Ida B. Wells was a bridge. Madame C.J. Walker was a bridge. Fannie Lou Hamer was a bridge. Every day that I'm out there I see myself as a resurrection of these women. I feel very strongly about black womanhood. And so if people interpret that I'm trying to be white because I try to speak well and do well in my life, it's insulting and myopic.''

These are strong words, but they are the words of experience and a strong inner capacity to go beyond the seeming restrictions of mortal capabilities. Oprah remembers the verbal cruelties that were thrust upon her by her classmates, and the rude ways she was treated by them. "No one's asked me about my psychological health at that time," Oprah revealed. "Frankly, I felt that most of the kids hated and resented me. They were into black power and anger. I was not. I guess that was because I was struggling just to be a human being. While they called me an 'Oreo', I remembered Jessie Jackson saying 'excellence is the deterrent to racism', so I pushed myself. In high school I was the teacher's pet, which created other problems. I never spoke in dialect—I'm not sure why, perhaps I was ashamed—and I was attacked for 'talking proper to white folks', for selling out.''

"I never talked about my feelings," she freely admits, "any more than I did when I was molested and raped, and then worried that a stomachache meant I was pregnant. Until my twenties, I never told a soul. My relationships with men were disastrous. Whenever I trusted someone, he abused me. It happened several times, even by my cousin's boyfriend. When I gathered my courage to tell my mother's side of the family the truth, they criticized me for airing my dirty laundry in public.'' Oprah kept her deeply felt emotions in check and did her best to try to forget. "There's only one way I've been able to survive being raped, molested, whipped, rejected . . . Only one way to cope with fears of pregnancy, my mother on welfare, my being fat and unpopular. As corny as this sounds," Oprah said, "my faith in God got me through. I am extremely spiritual. I've not gone into this before because it's personal, but faith is the core of my life."

Oprah talked to Norman King about the childhood rapes and abuse that she had experienced. "To Oprah," King recounted, "it seemed that neither of her parents wanted her. She reacted by behaving more and more badly. Then one night, a nineteen-year-old male cousin who frequently slept at Vernita Lee's apartment raped Oprah. She was too frightened to defend herself. 'I didn't tell anybody about it because I thought I would be blamed for it,' she said much later."

"As a result," King continued, "her behavior worsened. She lied, stayed out late, stole money from her mother's purse. She was also abused by other men, all of them 'trusted' family members or friends." Oprah remembers these cruel events regretfully. She recalls the hidden trauma and realizes that some of it is still present in her personality today.

She also has no problem remembering some of the other early influences that have had a long-term effect on her. Vernita Lee, Hattie Mae Lee, Vernon and Velma Winfrey— all are as much a part of Oprah Winfrey as her famous smile. Having pulled quite a few semi-rebellious stunts while living with her mother, Oprah can now see the far-reaching totality of it all. "I remember once," Oprah tells Susan Taylor, "I did this ridiculous thing. At thirteen, I saved up enough money to buy a dog, but my mother threatened to give him away for pooping on the floor."

"My mother said the puppy had to go," Oprah said another time. "And I thought if I could make the puppy look like a hero, I'd get to keep it. So I said, 'Mom, when I came home all the drawers were open, and the door was open, and things were hanging out of the drawers. And

Simone (Oprah's dog) was chasing these men down the
stairs. I think they were robbing us or something.' Now,
mind you, Simone was a tiny French poodle. And I thought,
'I've got to make it look like something's missing.' So I
threw my mother's jewelry out the window. I got in so
much trouble for that. It almost get me sent to a detention
home.''

''We even went down and filled out the papers, but
there wasn't room at the (detention) home. They said,
'You have to come back in two weeks.' My mother said,
'I can't have her another two weeks.' So Vernita Lee sent
Oprah to her father and stepmother.

Recently, Oprah told for the first time about the feelings
she had during her young life while going to school,
before Vernon was called to rear her. ''I was feeling a
sense of anguish,'' Oprah said of her multi-pressured youth.
''Because I was living with my mother in Milwaukee I
was in a situation where I was the only black kid, and I
mean the *only* one, in a school of 2,000 upper-middle-
class, suburban, Jewish kids. I would take the bus in the
morning to school with the maids who worked in their
homes.''

''I was going to this school because one of the teachers
in my inner-city school had seen me reading during my
lunch hour. My teachers started talking to me, saying 'You
need to get out of this environment.' When I changed
schools, I came to the understanding for the first time that
I was different and poor.''

''As long as no one tells you otherwise and you don't
see the other side, you're okay. But in that new school I
felt unimportant and insecure. So I'd make up stories and
lie to the kids about what my parents did. The life that I
saw these children lead was so totally different from what I
went home to, from what I was when I took the bus home
with the maids in the evening. I wanted my mother to be
like their mothers. I wanted my mother to have cookies
ready for me when I came home, and to say 'How was
your day?' But she was one of those maids. And she was

tired. And she was just trying to survive. Her way of showing love to me was getting out and going to work every day, putting clothes on my back, and having food on the table. At that time I didn't understand it. It's like when I was a kid, I used to watch *Leave It to Beaver,* and I noticed Beaver never got whippings. His parents always sat down and talked to him. June Cleaver,'' Oprah signs, ''has ruined a lot of us.''

''In the first grade,'' Oprah once said, ''six white kids were going to beat me up. So I told them about Jesus of Nazareth and what happened to the people who tried to stone him. The kids called me a preacher and left me alone after that.''

Oprah had her Biblical teachings down pat at this young age, just as she had mastered her early grade school curriculum. After completing her first grade studies easily, she was advanced to her school's third grade. This quick-leap technique stayed with Oprah for the next few decades, and it is with her today. Time seems to go at half-speed for Oprah Winfrey. She has accomplished more than most people can at twice her age. She was in third grade when the other children her age were still in the first. She had won a college scholarship at age sixteen to Tennessee State University. She graduated from T.S.U. and was hired by a major television network at the age of twenty-two. A few years later she had her own nationally syndicated talk show, two motion pictures under her belt, a third in the making, and a new situation comedy, loosely based on herself, which is in the process of being filmed.

It was just over a year ago that this young woman was hardly known to anyone outside the Chicago area. Now people from New York to Hawaii recognize her round, familiar face. ''I have a boundless energy,'' she says of her ability to do so many different projects in such a short amount of time while planning even more to keep her occupied in the future. Debbie DiMaio says that Oprah's ability to survive in the use-'em-and-lose-'em competitive arena of television comes from her industrial-strength stamina. "Her stamina," DiMaio says, "(is) mindboggling."

Oprah, as you have already learned, has had many a traumatic time on television and beyond. When the New York beauticians removed the hair from her deep-brown scalp, she was strong enough to swallow her anger and keep to her lengthy contract by sticking to her commitments. She could have sued the station and the beauticians, but that is not her style. As Dr. William Cox, Oprah's former drama coach, said to me, Oprah was always "too stubborn to quit until the job is done." Even with such a disturbing defacement as becoming bald, she still had a slight problem speaking out. "A New York beauty salon put some miracle ingredient on my hair that made me bald," she said comically. "I looked like Kojak. I was humiliated."

"I ended up in this place," Oprah recalled another time, "where they did chi-chi, poo-poo makeovers. They gave me a French perm. A French perm and Negro hair don't mix. I kept telling them, 'Excuse me, the lotion is beginning to burn a little.' It wasn't burning—it was flaming! But I was such a mouseburger that I sat there afraid to say anything."

The strengths that Oprah maintains are (and always have been) at least partially due to her father's influence. "I think the most important thing that my father did for me was exude a belief in himself," Oprah said to Susan Taylor of *Essence*. "A confidence in himself that I knew I could not override. I could not get away with anything, because when my father said something, he absolutely meant it."

When Oprah went to live with Vernon and Velma Winfrey, she was not at all like the little girl he had last seen on previous visits. She was heavily caked with loads of makeup, she wore tight short skirts and sexy tube tops, and she had a devilishly sly look in her eye that probably churned up Vernon's insides. She was bold and brass-sassy, and Vernon was about to show her who was boss.

Norman King wrote, "Vernon had become a successful businessman, opening a barber shop in 1964, and was now thinking of running a grocery store next to it. He had his own idea about how Oprah was going to behave—and war between them started immediately. When Oprah wore a dress that exposed her naked midriff, Vernon ordered her to change it. When she put on too much makeup, Vernon helped her rub it off. Whenever he caught her doing anything he did not approve of, he corrected her mercilessly. When she called him 'Pops', Verson said, "Oprah honey, I was 'Daddy' when you left and I'm going to be 'Daddy' since you're back. I will not accept the word 'Pops'!"

"She got the message. It was 'Daddy' from that day on. Vernon had another saying that she has never forgotten—his method of demanding quick obedience: "Listen girl, if I tell you a mosquito can pull a wagon, don't ask me no questions. Just hitch him up!" "He saved me," Oprah says. "He knew what he wanted and expected, and he would take nothing less."

Velma Winfrey, Oprah's stepmother, was as much a part of her Nus1ashville experience as Vernon. She also realized that Oprah needed a firm structuring from her as well as from her father. That way, no one person would be blamed for any punishment incurred. The two parents weren't security guards but rather more like in-home instructors. Since Vernon and Velma decided not to put Oprah's disciplinary instruction on just one pair of shoulders, they worked together for the mutual benefit of the family. Oprah told *Good Housekeeping* that her stepmother "was a very strong disciplinarian" and "I owe a lot to her."

"This is not acceptable," Vernon Winfrey stated, when his daughter came home with a report card full of C grades. "C is average," Oprah responded warmly; "this is not a bad grade." Vernon's simple, yet firm, reply to Oprah's statement revealed his disappointment. "If you were a child who could only get C's," he told her, "then that is all that I would expect of you. But you are not. And so in this house, for you," he stressed, "C's are not acceptable."

When Oprah's peers voted her the most popular girl in the school, during her sixteenth year, she was already well on her way to becoming the woman that she is today. The 'Grand Ole Oprah' slogan that she used to win her position on the school's student council is yet another early sign of her youthful wish for grandeur.

Oprah went with her father to Los Angeles when she was sixteen to speak at a large church function. While in Southern California, they had the opportunity to take a long, leisurely stroll down Hollywood Boulevard. When Oprah saw the famous stars' names in the sidewalk, and the fancy stars in the cement, she said to her father, "One day, I'm going to put my star beside those other stars!" Vernon silently acknowledged Oprah's statement as they strolled over the famous names.

Like any other celebrity, Oprah has people that like her and people who don't. To some she is a friend; to others she is an accomplished actress, a talk-show host, and a pest. She's been called a 'Black Mammy', 'next-door neighbor' and 'Aunt Jemima'; sexy, exploitative, and kind. To some viewers she is a peer counselor. No matter what you think of her, she is still going to be Oprah Winfrey. No one can take that away from her. At times, she can be a quiet friend; at other times, a champion of human rights. There is really no one around who does the kind of things that she does.

There are not many black people who would sit around and talk with a group of Ku Klux Klan women, nor are there many who would sit and talk with the Klan's Grand Dragon. Oprah has done both. "It was as if the burden of every black person was on my back," Oprah said, recalling her somewhat frightening encounter with the Grand Dragon.

One of the most intriguing programs that Oprah attempted was when she packed up the show and went to racism-torn Forsythe County, Georgia. The program was exciting and emotionally wrought. Forsythe County was described by Oprah as the "current battlefield of the civil rights movement." Many recent demonstrations have taken place there over the past months.

"You are looking at a land in America," Oprah began as she stood in the middle of the invisible and visible chaos, "where not single black person has lived in seventy-five years. We watched as thousands marched in this town to shouts of 'Nigger, go home.' We came here today not to argue whether black people have a right to be here—the Civil Rights Act guarantees them that right—we are here to try to understand the attitudes and motivations of those who threw rocks at the recent demonstrations." Oprah's executive producer said of the trip, "We want to do more shows with that kind of style." The trip to all-white Forsythe County was just another example of Oprah's willingness to confront any pressing issue head on.

She still hasn't endeared herself to everyone yet, though. David Letterman still makes jibes about her. "I like the old Oprah better," said Letterman on *Late Night*. He said that now she looks too much like Diana Ross. He also said that after losing so much weight, she looks like she could be "a waitress at the Metro Bowl." According to David Letterman, Oprah should return to her former self when she looked like "Mrs. Butterworth." Though Oprah is responsible for most of what is said about her weight, she sometimes isn't ready to hear the cold jabs from people who want to joke about it until she hurts. David Letterman just sees Oprah as a fat woman to make fun of.

Others dislike her for even talking about her weight. They say that she has developed an obsession with her weight and with food, and that her dieting habits take up too much of her converstion. Oprah doesn't see it that way. In fact, she says that she doesn't talk about her weight any more than any other overweight person. "It *is* an obsession," Oprah declares angrily. "It is all any overweight woman talks about. It just happens that I'm in the public eye, so people think I talk about it more."

She has recently lost many pounds, and this is now a dominant feature of her mind-set on her show and at personal appearances. As always, she brings what is on her mind into the topics of her conversation. Then, every word she utters is scrutinized carefully for faults and blunders. She will endure, though, and the jokes she has to put up with will ensure her the last laugh.

Charles Whitaker said, "She rules over the blue and gray set on which the show is played like a combination of Barbara Walters and Joan Rivers. One minute she's all quips and one-liners, the next minute she's eliciting painful and personal testimonies from guests or celebrities. She also reveals her own personal tragedies. In the past, she has recounted her failing relationships, a childhood episode of sexual abuse, and her constant battle to lose weight. These insights have endeared her to Americans, making her one of the most sought-after speakers in the country."

"*The Oprah Winfrey Show* production office at WLS-TV in Chicago is cluttered with books, recordings, telephones, files, flowers, stuffed animals," notes Leslie Rubinstein. "There are Christmas Seal awards, a Girl Scout plate, the Good News Bible, and an Emmy for the teenage special, *Survival, Everything to Live For*."

"Stars have wandered in and out of Oprah's office," Rubinstein says. "But what the Oprah Winfrey Show does is 'get-'em-in-the-gut' show topics: sexual disorders, battered wives, self-mutilation, people who hate overweight people, people who hate their bosses, how to find a man, men who pay for sex. Nothing is taboo."

Oprah wasn't always as self-assured as she is today. Her early years were a learning phase, and Oprah soon discovered it would be difficult to find television work that would fit her personality. "I was so naive," Oprah once said of her novice years on television. "I thought you could just go on the air and do the best you could." But as much as Oprah tried to be herself, to *allow* herself to be herself, the sorrier the result. As difficult as it was for her, and as much as she wanted to succeed, she still couldn't bring herself to appear on the screen as her higher-ups wanted her to appear. Her writing was very poor, and she just didn't have it in her to do intensified research while working on a story.

It was also difficult for her to come up with a clear, finished news story. She was often emotionally effected by truly touching stories, becoming too involved with them. "If the story was too sad . . . I'd have to fight back the tears," she recalls. Eventually, and gradually, Oprah began to 'wing-it' on the air, much to the displeasure of her bosses. "I'd be reading something and break in to say, 'Wow, that's terrible!' My reactions were getting to be real. It was a kick with me."

When Oprah was still a teen, Vernon Winfrey talked her into entering beauty pageants. The first was sponsored by the Elks Club, and Oprah won it hands down. The prize was a four-year scholarship to Tennessee State University. When Vernon talked her into entering another contest, she won by using her own merits and intuitive honesty. She was, at one point, about to tell the judges that she wanted to become a fourth grade teacher, but what actually came out of her mouth was, "I believe in truth, so I want to be a journalist." Her spontaneous reaction kept her in the running.

The judges tried to find out more about the few finalists, so they asked each of the girls what she would do if she had a million dollars to spend any way she wanted. Of course the other girls said that they'd donate the money to many worthy charitable foundations or causes. But not Oprah Winfrey. She came right out and told the startled judges, "If I had a million dollars, I'd be a spending fool!" Her humorous honesty made the judges choose her as the winner. Little did they know that the thin young beauty who stood before them would become one of America's brightest new stars and one of television's richest personalities. They did, to their credit, see some of her special qualities; they saw something in her that made them realize she was much more than a pretty face.

Later on, other people in prominent positions began to take notice of her obvious talents. Potential was practically oozing out of her. Dennis Swanson clearly saw her attributes and boldly put Oprah's show opposite Phil Donahue's. It was an incredible longshot, but Swanson took the chance. His idea turned out to be a winner. Norman King once said that "Oprah vowed not to cower in Donahue's shadow and knew that she'd have to impress her own style on the show to make it fit her."

The results of Swanson's gamble were amazing. *The Oprah Winfrey Show* beat Donahue by so much that for every one person who watched Phil Donahue's program, there were two who watched Oprah's show.

"Girl," Oprah used to tell herself, "look at you! You're not on the farm in Mississippi feeding those hogs no more!"

It was immediately clear that Oprah was going to be a raging success and that her career would continue to soar. Even *The Washington Post*, which is known for its critical views and biting commentary, raved about her, and continues to do so today, calling her "The zaftig gab queen" who sent "poor yakked-out Donahue into video menopause."

"ABC is negotiating with her production company to develop a situation comedy to star Ms. Winfrey," says Charles Whitaker. "In it, she will play—what else?—a single talk-show host who lives in Chicago." The comedy program will be shot in Chicago while Oprah continues with her show and the dozens of other projects with which she occupies her time. Oprah says that there will be no problem doing all of her projects at once, and that none of them will suffer for it. "I have a boundless energy," says Oprah.

Her newest project, *The Women of Brewster Place*, will be shown on ABC-TV in the spring of 1988. By then there will be very few people in America who have never heard of Oprah Winfrey. "I want to be a great actress," she smiled. "It's a glorious time for me. I'm doing exactly what I wanted to be doing at age 33. I feel I'm ripening, coming into my own. It's an exciting time, an exciting age."

Oprah spoke of what she is trying to do with her show and what she is trying to say to her audience. "It's kind of a spiritual message," she says. "If you watch the program for a period of time, it's transmitted again and again. The message is: You are responsible for your life. People watch the show and realize that they're not alone. Whatever problem you have, there's somebody out there who has overcome something like it."

"I used to create situations that were a direct reflection of what was going on in my head: my self-doubts, my own insecurities and discomfort. God was trying to show me that I was who I was because that's who I chose to be, and God was saying that when I chose to be something different, then I would have something different. And that's exactly what happened."

"One thing I have in common with the character Sofia in *The Color Purple* is that I have decided that what people think of me isn't any of my business. If I can just do what Paul says in the Bible, press to the mark of the high calling of God, then I will have done what I am supposed to do."

Today Oprah Winfrey looks out of her high-rise picture windows and watches over her adopted hometown, Chicago. There is much to remember and many things to come. The future is a treasure chest from God, and hers is almost halfway open. Oprah Winfrey's final chapter is, as yet, unwritten.

BIBLIOGRAPHY

Books:

Bergman, Peter, *The Negro in America*, Harper and Row, 1969.

Naylor, Gloria, *The Women of Brewster Place*, Penguin Books, 1983.

Waldron, Robert, *Oprah!*, St. Martin's Press, 1987.

Newspapers and Periodicals:

Anderson, Chris, "Meet Oprah Winfrey," *Good Housekeeping* (August 1986).

Ann Landers (October 1986).

Barthel, Joan, "Here Comes Oprah," *Ms. Magazine* (1986).

Christopher, Mark, "Yakking Is Cheap in the War of the Mouths," *Los Angeles Times/San Francisco Chronicle* (Nov. 3, 1986).

"Dionne Warwick Wins NAACP 'Image' Award," *United Press International/San Francisco Chronicle* (Dec. 7, 1986).

Edwards, Audrey, "Oprah Winfrey—Stealing the Show," *Essence* (October 1986).

117

Frank, Allan Dodds and Sweig, Jason, "The Fault Is Not in Our Stars," *Forbes* (Sept. 1987).

Grossberger, Lewis, "Can We Not Talk?" *Rolling Stone* (Dec. 1986).

Harmetz, Aljean, "Spielberg Is Honored by Directors," *New York Times* (March 10, 1986).

Johns, Pamela, "Fine Tuning," *Essence* (July 1985).

King, Norman, "Oprah," *Good Housekeeping* (Aug. 1987).

Mansfield, Stephanie, "Now Everyone Can Schmoose with Oprah," *Washington Post/San Francisco Chronicle* (Nov. 11, 1986).

Morgan, Thomas, "Troubled Girl's Evolution into an Oscar Nominee," *New York Times* (March 4, 1986).

"Oprah Winfrey's Success Story," *Ladies Home Journal* (March 1987).

Parade Magazine (dates unknown).

Robertson, Nan, "Actress' Varied Roads to *The Color Purple*," *New York Times* (Feb. 13, 1986).

Rubinstein, Leslie, "Oprah!" *McCalls* (Aug. 1987).

Schine, Cathleen, "Oprah Winfrey: She Believes," *Vogue* (May 1986).

Stinton, Michael, "Oprah's Revamp," *Star* (Sept. 29, 1987).

Taylor, Susan L., "An Intimate Talk with Oprah," *Essence* (Aug. 1987).

Waters, Harry (with Patricia King), "Chicago's Grand New Oprah," *Newsweek* (Dec. 31, 1984).

Witaker, Charles, "T.V.'s Most Talented Talk Show Host," *Ebony* (March 1987).

Witaker, Charles, "T.V.'s New Daytime Darling," *The Saturday Evening Post,* (August 1987).

Reference:
Current Biography (March 1987).

Television:
60 Minutes, 1986.
   Dolly!, 1987.
   Late Night with David Letterman, October 1987.
   The Late Show, 1987.
   The Oprah Winfrey Show, King World Synd., 1987.